Especially
for
Janet Angelone
Thank you
for
reading &
sharing.

~ Jean
Baker

Schizophrenia:

Evolving from My Son's Suicide to the Classroom

A mother relates her life experience with her son's
mental illness and translates that knowledge to the
special education classroom.

JEAN BAKER

with writings by

BRIAN CASE

Dedication

This book is dedicated to the memory of my son Brian Case and to numerous others who struggle with schizophrenia as well as many other forms of mental illness.

Brian at age 16 when he still appeared to be mentally healthy. Photo was taken in our front yard in Park City..

Disclaimer

I have attempted to recreate events, thoughts, feelings and perspectives from my personal memories. Brian's writings were acquired directly from his own letters, poetry and notebooks. In order to maintain their anonymity in some instances, I may have changed or omitted names of individuals, places, or other identifying characteristics and details in order to protect the identities of those involved. This book is in no way intended to be used or suggested as replacement for professional medical advice, care or treatment. If anyone who reads this material or has awareness of others who need treatment, please do not hesitate to seek medical and legal assistance.

Acknowledgments

I feel gratitude beyond recognition to my husband Jim, to my sons Dillon and Cody, and to the rest of my family for their continued love and support. I appreciate so much the friends who stood staunchly beside me through these years during all phases of joy and grief. I also honor all parents, families and educators who live in the trenches and continually support their loved ones and students despite the everyday struggles and turmoil of mental illness. I realize I was incredibly fortunate to have so much love and support. I cannot comprehend how others have survived with so little. My heart goes out to you, those who continue the struggle, for all your dedication and for never giving up the fight. This book is for you. If we all speak for their shamed silence, there will be no more ignorance. A portion of all proceeds will be used toward educating others to eradicate the stigma of mental illness.

Schizophrenia: In Brian's own words

I was trapped inside a very small bubble,

oblivious to my yearning for oxygen,

and I could not understand this predicament

for the life of myself.

Nor could I smile, nor dance,

nor could I stretch my arms widespread,

like Jesus, below the sun.

And tragically old in the prime of my youth,

I'm strangling myself as I am lowered

below the open night within my coffin,

my own devise, into the hell I could never conceive,

and I see the other children dancing around my plot,

the stars reflected off their pupils, smiling.

It never once occurred to me that I was dying–

my rage corrupted my eyes.

At least I was freed, inside my bubble, of reality..

Suicide Survivor

As we planned his funeral, I reluctantly sat down at my computer to write Brian's obituary for the local newspaper. Inexplicably, Brian's own words jumped out at me on the monitor. A moment earlier, my sister had been composing her thoughts on the computer and had no logical explanation as to why or how his testimony suddenly materialized. At the time, I was hysterical, thinking he had just been in the room and typed the lines. Now I wonder at the insightful message he left for us to decipher.

THE OBITUARY: BRIAN CASE

Beloved son and brother, Brian Case, age 21, Park City resident, passed on to his Heavenly Father May 5, 1999 in Austin, Texas in a drowning incident. He was a 1996 graduate of Park City High School and attended the University of Utah. Brian loved life, family, friends, music, poetry, skiing, fishing, mountain biking and running through the mountains. He was well-loved and will be missed.

There was not one crystal clear moment when I realized something was truly wrong with my perfect son. His biologic brain disease, *schizophrenia*, evolved rather like fragmented pieces of incidents lost in a timeless blur. As I begin writing his story, it has been a few years since Brian's death, and I am compelled to try to put the mysterious pieces of his life together and make some sense out of the chaos. I hope that

SCHIZOPHRENIA:

Brian's twin brothers will have a more comprehensive perspective of the actual events before his death. Eventually, I believe family members will also acquire deeper insight into the complexity of his illness. More importantly, other parents, friends and families, or medical, legal and educational professionals will benefit from reading Brian's story and will have a greater understanding of the stigma of mental illness and how it steals the lives of those we love.

May 5, 2000 – First Anniversary of Brian's Suicidal Death

Jim and I took the day off work and visited Red Butte Gardens on the high bench above Salt Lake City. Today was the first anniversary of Brian's death, and I could just barely stand the loss. Sometimes it still hurt to breathe, and I habitually looked for him in crowds or expected him to walk in the door late at night. I still do.

On this first anniversary, I felt that although my life had been shattered by his suicide, I was starting to recover some sense of normalcy. A day at this beautiful park reminded me that life goes on whether we're ready or not. Since the Great Salt Lake pre-historically was once much deeper, this area would have been the beach. It is a place Brian loved, where we once took long walks and had serious talks. I remember the wooden bench where we sat in the shade one hot summer afternoon. He told me he couldn't stay in college following his freshman year. He planned to "write music and poetry and read a lot," he said. My breath stopped. I worried that if something happened to me or if I died suddenly, Brian would be unemployable, homeless, and living in the street. He was nineteen that summer.

Today, May 5th, was the actual one-year anniversary of his death, as far as the police could determine. Contrary to the original obituary, he had remained in the lake in Austin for five days before his body was found. Our lives will never be the same. I will try to retrace my memory of what actually happened to Brian and how he died. It is the only salvation for my sanity to analyze and try to understand. By not acknowledging his existence or talking about him, I have learned the hard pain of burying my feelings to spare others. More importantly, I hope it will give someone else an understanding that will help eliminate the ignorance and out-dated stigma of mental illness and suicide.

4

Within a few weeks, I realized my closest friends and family had no concept of the pain we were suffering. At Christmas, a good friend sent an e-mail that joked about different types of mental illness. An apology quickly followed, that it was sent "all in fun" to everyone on her list. She'd forgotten we might be sensitive to such a tasteless parody. I wondered if she considered apologizing to everyone on her list. Would she be amused if I joked about child molestation or abuse which would hit home for her? Is it okay to ridicule a handicapped person for something they cannot help, if they are crippled by birth, accident or disease?

Or what if a perfect child is born with a time bomb that goes off in his brain at 16? Is it more acceptable to laugh at someone who is ill above the neck rather than below? One day at lunch, another friend said she was very irritated that our young male waiter was clueless, repeating the order, appearing confused, not moving quickly enough. She was adamant we not leave him a tip after lunch. I felt so sad as tears burned my eyes. He responded exactly as Brian would have, the further his illness progressed. Brian struggled with bussing tables at twenty-one. He'd been so bright at fourteen, he had attended a special session of environmental science at the University of Utah.

I visited my parents in Texas two months after Brian's death, but they didn't mention our loss until I brought up the subject on the fourth day of our stay. I asked my father, "So what about Brian?" And he responded, "What about Brian?" The closest neighbors had not been told. A year and a half later, a next door neighbor, a nurse who saw them weekly, asked me how Brian was doing. She remembered him as a child who had played at her house with her children. She had no idea that he had died. My mother said she didn't see the neighbor very often and had forgotten to mention what happened to Brian.

Another incidence of family denial occurred when I visited Houston and met my sister's new husband. As he drove me to the airport after my visit, I gingerly brought up the topic and asked if he knew about Brian. I began talking about the time Brian had spent in Texas with my sister and how much I missed him since his death. My brother-in-law seemed confused, saying it was healthy for young people to get out and travel. I thought he had to be an idiot to conclude Brian had merely gone on a walkabout. When I told him what had actually happened, he was amazed to learn that Brian had been diagnosed with schizophrenia. In turn, I was amazed that this man had married into my family, and that bit of recent family history had never been mentioned to him.

I stay awake many nights replaying the events of the past five years like an old movie I've seen a thousand times. I fall asleep early, only to stay in a deep sleep for a few hours. Then I awaken and remain sleepless from one or two in the morning until four or five a.m. Lack of sleep is less difficult now than it was at first. I may have just adapted to less sleep with the stream of thoughts that flows through my brain all night.

At first, I heard Brian crying as a baby. I would sit bolt upright from my sleep, thinking I must go see the baby. As weeks and months passed, I would look up and see a shadow round a corner as if Brian was still a toddler hiding from me. I thought I would lose my mind. In many complicated dreams, I would be trying to rescue him from danger. Now I picture him at different stages of his life, mostly fond memories and happy smiles.

Grief can affect so many thoughts and feelings. It can make you wish you could go where your loved one has gone. There are stages of anger when you are mad at them for leaving you behind to suffer alone. The obsession of the loss can steal your life as you go through your days numbly, as if in a coma. Then, slowly, most survivors I've met begin coming back to life, although it may take years, even decades. The term *suicide survivor* sounds like a contradiction in terms. The victim didn't survive but we, the family, did survive—sort of. We take each day one step at a time like an addict; we are addicted to the pain of our loss.

FROM THE BEGINNING

I've learned that many schizophrenics are born in the spring and some experts believe there is a virus-related influence to the timing of these births. Not so with Brian. I remember the elation I felt when I realized I was pregnant in early February. This baby was the result of a planned Christmas promise earlier in December. I was a school teacher and having the baby would eventually mean a long term postponement of my teaching career. At that time in the 70's, I didn't even consider that

I ever wanted to choose a career over children and a family. After seven years of marriage and struggling for both of us to complete college, I was thrilled to be able to stay home and be a full time mommy. Unlike the rest of the world, as was becoming the common societal trend at the time, leaving my baby in daycare was not likely to happen. Fortunately, my husband's job with the government meant we could live with a certain sense of security, though modestly. Incredibly, at that time, our income was $12,000 per year with a home mortgage of $150 for a house that cost $30,000.

Brian arrived on a bright October day in 1977, at Woman's Hospital in Baton Rouge, Louisiana, with no real complications. We'd checked into the hospital the evening before and been told my condition was false labor. We were abruptly instructed to return in two weeks and summarily dismissed. I recall crying in the parking lot with my very frustrated husband, not yet thirty years old, yelling that he was embarrassed that even after taking Lamaze classes, I didn't know what I was doing. Writing this now, the scene is almost comical. My husband and a couple of young male interns were giving me grief for not knowing how far I had dilated. After leaving the hospital, the event smoothed over with a movie and a cheeseburger, although that was the last thing I should have eaten prior to childbirth. It was Saturday night and the opening of the movie *Star Wars*. I must have gotten up from my theater seat a dozen times to use the restroom, while thinking I would never be able to stand the burning sensations and pressure for another two weeks. Essentially, I was going through labor in a movie theater. The plot made absolutely no sense to me but, ironically, the movie later became Brian's all time favorite, complete with birthday party themes, costumes, toys, and eventually, sequels.

At this point, I'll call my now ex-husband "Sam" for the sake of privacy and convenience. Sam and I drove home, barely speaking. I don't remember sleeping at all that night although my husband fell into a sound sleep. By five a.m., I awakened him and insisted the baby was ready to be born. He was grouchy and in no mood to drive back to the hospital. Eventually, with my threat of calling a taxi, I persuaded him to get dressed and drive.

Brian came into the world at 7:05 a.m. with an impatient lusty cry, red hair and wrinkly skin. His eyes were a startling blue and seemed to have all the wisdom of an old man. That same evening, the nurse called from the nursery and asked if she should bring Brian to us as he was crying heartily. Since Sam was watching football on tv, he placed the baby in the crook of his arm, and father and son enjoyed the game without another whimper out of the newborn. It was the oddest thing that the little guy was already adapting to sports in an effort to please his father on the first day of his life. Decades later, as an adult, I recall Brian saying his father could only express love from the sidelines of a field. Sam's own father, an alcoholic war hero, had flown from other countries just to watch him play baseball as a boy. This was the role model my ex-husband used unvaryingly throughout his life.

When we brought him home, Brian, as an infant, could not be easily soothed. I could not believe how other mothers talked about their babies sleeping through the night. Although I breastfed him for a total of eighteen months, he cried frequently from what our pediatrician thought was colic. I also suspected he really didn't like being alone all night and cried out for companionship. We traveled from Louisiana to East Texas for Brian's christening when he was six weeks old. My dad walked him in circles around the living room, the baby held over his strong arm, until Grandpa joked he'd worn out the carpet on his first grandson.

With my best friend, Mary, also a teacher and a new mom, we took our babies out almost daily. Brian loved the bright lights and excitement of visiting the mall or even riding in the baby seat on the back of my bicycle. Compared to the crying days of staying at home when I would end up crying, too, the stimulation of being out in the world seemed to mellow his moods. Those were the happiest days in Louisiana.

Within a year, we'd followed Sam's career and moved to the Black Hills of South Dakota. The only way to get Brian to nap at all was in his car seat after a short ride. I couldn't even place him in his crib without awakening him so I remained in the car, parked in the driveway while he slept, both of us exhausted. My husband had business trips back East for as long as three weeks, resulting in my near complete isolation. In my reclusive world, the few neighbors in the little mountain area commuted fifteen miles to Rapid City, busy with their days at work. One neighbor had frantically called me over because her baby was turning blue. The baby died soon after the ambulance came. This tragic occurrence caused me to worry even more about our remote location and Brian's continual illnesses.

In contrast, Sam loved coming home, playing his guitar on the deck and surveying his expansive domain, our ten acres bordered by National Forest land. He thoroughly enjoyed bragging to his peers in Washington, D.C. about his ten acres in the Black Hills. He was not home when the driveway was literally buried in snow and temperatures dropped to sixty below zero that winter.

For me, it was difficult to make friends or get to town very often. It was the late seventies when gasoline prices had suddenly doubled. The only real relationship I had was with our pediatrician whom I saw regularly due to Brian's chronic ear infections. I began to think I was in trouble mentally, longing for my next appointment with my baby's doctor and an opportunity to visit town. There were days and days of Brian's crying with his ear problems until I thought I'd lose my mind. I remember thinking if I physically threw myself through the huge plate glass window, someone might pay attention to this depression that I was sinking into or understand that I desperately needed contact with the outside world. I imagined the guys in white coats and a van coming to get me and haul me away. I felt so ashamed that I couldn't handle the isolation better. My mother wisely told me to find ways to get out, get to town and get involved. She suggested that I teach my son everything I could and that became my purpose in life. As he grew a little older, he became my fellow explorer, soul mate companion and the center of my mommy universe.

During that year, I finally saw a counselor who, unfortunately, was not much help. He insisted I needed to learn to meditate and taught me some chants. What I didn't feel I needed was more introspective time alone. When he met with me and my husband, they discussed sports and sex, and basically agreed through male bonding that my problems were unrelated to the marriage. It was 1978 and a rather thoroughly dominated male world, after all. I felt alone, misunderstood and betrayed.

I had struggled with what I thought was "normal" depression through my teens and early adulthood. As a sensitive young girl, I had been date raped and had never sought counseling or any emotional support at the time. I could not imagine sharing the pain with my parents or even admitting that I believed I loved someone who could hurt me so much. A decade later, my husband was the only person with whom I'd been able to share my painful secret. I assumed it was one of those unfortunate bumps on life's road that had to be accepted and survived alone. In retrospect, I now realize that as a teen and young adult, I had continually felt extreme anxiety over grade performance, lack of self-esteem over social performance and general paranoia over an entire list of other issues. All of these anxieties became intensified and magnified after Brian's death.

BRIAN'S CHILDHOOD YEARS

I struggled through the isolation of living in the Black Hills a year before we sold the house and acreage to a couple from New York City. We moved into Rapid City, and I quickly adjusted by joining women's support clubs and children's play groups. The sudden change in my social environment put me in a whirlwind of friendships and activities. It seemed my old depression was a situational thing of the past.

Somehow I managed the courage to visit the local School of Mining and Technology and talk to the retiring English professor, Mrs. Jeanette Kinyon. I told her how seriously I wanted to be a writer. Although I had a degree in English Literature, somewhere my education had failed to put me on the path to actually writing anything beyond school papers. Baffled, she hardly hesitated to pull out an index card and make a list of steps that actually were common sense but helped me tremendously. I went home and began working on the first notation on the card. Over the next few years, she became my mentor and often entertained us in her home. She adored Brian's childish antics and even served him tea and cookies on her collection of fine china.

Craving knowledge, I took on the task of commuting sixty miles to Spearfish, South Dakota, to acquire teacher certification. During this time, I had two miscarriages and finally dropped out of classes. The depression returned with a vengeance. My husband was frustrated that I was not fulfilling his expectations of the stay at home mom he'd bargained for originally. Much later, I was not the financially achieving career woman he wished for, either.

Brian, now two years old, reverted to diapers after being potty trained and still suffered with hearing problems. The pediatrician rudely suggested I was being "trendy" to ask about an ear operation for my son. This was definitely the end of my daydream relationship with this insensitive doctor. An ear specialist immediately recommended tubes in Brian's ears which cleared up the problems completely. I will never forget him as a toddler, smacking his open palm on the glass door and asking, "What noise?" This was the first time he'd heard the birds chirping in the yard. With the improvement in hearing, Brian's speech advanced overnight so that he was talking constantly, asking questions and demanding answers. He had so much catching up to do and unquenchable curiosity to learn about everything around him. He was also developing quite a sense of humor and constantly entertained us with his amazing antics. Being his mother and companion was a full time, challenging job as well as being a rewarding one. I remember especially mischievous events such as his coloring the neighbor's houses with a green marker about two feet from the ground. While I'd been on the phone with my sister, and Sam was downstairs watching tv, Brian had managed to get the front door unlocked, travel the neighborhood and cross a busy street to a house that had big wheel toys in the backyard. When I followed the trail of green marker and found him, he was happily playing and gave me a gigantic grin. Overall, he was such a good kid, the necessity for discipline was rare and minimal.

He was also such a cute kid. Once when he was sitting in a restaurant highchair, playing and laughing, a waitress in Galveston ran her cart into the wall while smiling at him. He resembled Ron Howard as "Opey" with a smattering of freckles on an upturned nose, sparkling blue eyes and a mop of reddish blonde hair. I have often thought that God made Brian especially good-looking so that it was some compensation for his mental illness. People react positively to someone who looks healthy and attractive.

Brian at age 2, riding on Grandpa's shoulders,
the safest place in the world.

Unfortunately, good looks can also be a negative aspect because a healthy looking person is considered lazy if they're non-productive, unemployed and mentally ill. As Brian became an adult, being hand-some wasn't an asset in getting the help he needed. His eyes were a startling blue/turquoise color with an inset ring of gold around the pupil that always attracted females. As he grew older, with his sandy blonde hair, high cheekbones and broad smile, he gave the illusion of being a hearty Irishman. We have a tintype photo, the spitting image of Brian, of a relative who emigrated from Ireland.

SURPRISE TWIN BROTHERS - ALBUQUERQUE

By the time Brian reached age three, we'd followed Sam's career to Albuquerque, New Mexico in my eighth month of pregnancy. Although I did not realize we were expecting surprise twins, Brian consistently told strangers we were having "two babies." He was jumping up and down at the hospital waiting room, telling everyone, "I told you it was two babies!" There was never a more proud or helpful big brother. The photos from that time are some of the most precious ones of our lives. We were now a complete family of five.

A few years later, Brian developed terrible nightmares and bedwetting problems that continued through age six. Eventually, he could stay dry all night, but his touch with reality was always confused by his wild imagination. One night terror that I remember had him sitting upright in bed and screaming loudly. I held him and asked who I was, and he began crying, "You're my mom." Later, he told me he'd dreamed of dinosaurs that were chasing him.

However, in cleaning the garage more recently, I came across some of his high school papers. This particular one drew my interest. It is a review of Vonnegut's "Slaughter House Five." Brian wrote in his junior year in high school:

The power of a book is as much disciplined from the author as it is absorbed through the reader. Perhaps this is why they say there are two sides to every story. For me, the story drew far further than a flat page with flat words. One of my special qualities is to develop pop-up books—to bring fiction to reality. After all, what really is reality? I am one of the few to experience night terrors, which are far more real, insane, vivid and alive than nightmares. One night, while I acquired a fever, I screamed as I watched my mother die. She was holding me and rocking me in my bed, and I knew it. But I am insane during these terrors, and there is no reason why my mother cannot die on a battlefield while tucking me into bed and attempting to awaken me from a bad dream. There was no bad dream, however, for reality and fiction were mixed into a melting pot of insanity. There were no rules. Thanks to these night terrors, I have experienced the deaths of nearly every person I have ever known, and I do mean I have experienced it. I have heard

from older people, on occasion, that teenagers think they are immortal.
I tell these respectable people that adolescents are not idiots, for they do
know what death is. They have not, however, dreamt enough.

Sometimes I will suddenly remember one of his perplexed expressions or confused statements that didn't seem so alarming at the time. In retrospect, I can identify obscure pieces of Brian's broken life. In his early teens, he came home from a Boy Scout campout with some absurd story about the scoutmaster getting angry and throwing rocks at the boys while out in the desert. I thought Brian must have had a bad dream or his imagination was on some childish spin. The scoutmaster was a stern, older man who would be an unlikely candidate for throwing rocks at kids. Brian was just short of becoming an eagle scout when he dropped out of the program.

Years later, I recalled that his first grade teacher in New Mexico had called me at work and insisted I should do something about Brian's lack of focus in school. When we had moved late in my pregnancy from Rapid City to Albuquerque, I remember trying to give Brian as much attention as possible before the twins' delivery. By the time he was in first grade, he was a very responsible big brother to his twin brothers. My first response to the teacher's accusation was one of self-defense in feeling attacked that she was so abrupt and insistent. She'd called me at work during the day when I couldn't possibly concentrate on the problem or discuss the matter. For six months, I had tried to work full time at a university, placing myself in full time guilt and anger over trying to do it all. I drove ten miles across the Rio Grande in Albuquerque where I placed my twin three-year-olds in daycare while Brian was in school. Before and after school, he stayed with Shellee, a close friend who provided daycare with several other children in her home.

I finally confronted Sam with the news that I could not continue working a full time day job, raising three young sons and maintaining our home alone while he often traveled eighty percent of the time. He reacted by talking of returning to college to study water law but found another route to escape home life in real estate sales. If it had not been for the boys, I've often thought we would have divorced during the financial stress at that time.

Fortunately for Brian, school had gone fairly smoothly in second and third grades as he adapted and seemed to settle into meeting the school's expectations. Ironically, he became a leader that the other kids easily followed. He joined Boy Scouts, took karate and swimming lessons, attended religious classes, even served as an altar boy, and played soccer and baseball. I remember that at his First Communion ceremony, he held the little prayer book up to the other kids, saying, "These are the rules. You have to follow all these rules." Everyone smiled.

When I had other parent/teacher conferences, I learned that Brian was distracted at school and very often on another planet, as the teachers put it. Since his father was a distracted scientist and a space cadet himself, I had come to think this was just normal behavior for the two of them. According to my own observation, Brian was unusually bright, could converse with adults on many topics and seemed mature beyond his years. In preschool, he'd excelled at learning to read and developing abstract ideas. Sometimes his mind was on the stars and planets, but he still responded to the questions I asked. I decided his teachers were wrong. I lived to regret that I hadn't listened more closely.

The disagreements with his teachers were the beginning for me of what I felt the schools were lacking in insight. Over the last three decades, I've found many parents who agree. It seemed to us that if a child was in any way different, then it was inconvenient for the educational system to deal with students who did not conform to their expectations. Their approach felt like accusations and attacks on my parenting. My experience indicated that Brian was very bright and learned quickly. When he became bored, he did mentally escape to another realm. Although I'd taught regular classes of seventh and eighth graders in a Catholic School in Louisiana, I had not been specifically trained to recognize that Brian might have some type of learning problems. Belatedly, I now have that training that I use everyday in the special ed classroom.

The magnitude of Brian's problem was brought home to me years later when he was a freshman at the University of Utah. I was standing outside his college dorm when Brian explained he could not concentrate on his classes. I suggested strongly that if he didn't smoke weed, he could probably focus better. Then he began screaming at me that he had been tested at the university counseling for ADD, for attention deficit problems, and demanded to know why I hadn't taken care of the problem when he was young. He was now nineteen the spring of his freshman year when this incident occurred. If only things had been that simple, I realized later.

*Brian seemed extremely silly and normal in this photo
at age 8 in Albuquerque, NM.*

When we moved from Albuquerque to Park City, Utah, Brian was near the end of third grade. He had a terrible time adjusting and kept asking me if it was okay if he left school and came home because our new home was within walking distance. He truly missed his life and friends in Albuquerque. To deal with his loss, he began building a "time machine" in a nearby field and talked constantly of going back to his former school and friends.

I recently found an old notebook of Brian's that indicated his insecurities as early as November 6, 1987, the fall following our move to Park City.

I changed so I was different from others. I lived in New Mexico. All the kids thought I was smart and knew a lot about water and rocks. My best friend was Jimmy who moved to the same town and at the same time. I was four and he was three. We knew each other and became good friends. By the time I was eight years old my mom said we would probably move in a year. That is when my worries began. What if I can't make friends if I move?

There were other instances when he seemed out of touch with reality. At nine years old, he still was adamant there was a Santa Claus and would fight to the death for this belief. Park City kids who were a bit more worldly and well-traveled, openly ridiculed his belief. It didn't help that at Christmas, my parents had continued to foster this idea with Santa ringing bells and leaving sleigh tracks in the yard. When I finally told Brian there was a "spirit" of Christmas, he over-reacted angrily. He quickly concluded these "lies" covered the tooth fairy, the Easter bunny, etc. I thought he would never stop crying, and he didn't speak to me for days. This was another flaw in his understanding of reality and fantasy. I felt like a monster.

SPORTS PRESSURE

Even before we moved away from Albuquerque and upset his world, there had been a problem with Brian's involvement in sports. His habit of staring into space as the ball sailed by was a point of contention with his father. Sam, who had wanted to play semi-professional baseball himself, had no patience for his son's lack of ability or attention. His unreasonable expectations took over his common sense in trying to turn Brian into an athlete. The boy was a mixture of his mother's lack of coordination and his father's absent-minded professor mentality. Still, his father made no effort to hide his anger, disappointment and frustration, often loudly yelling at his son from the sidelines. Sam frequently became verbally abusive, sometimes using profanity during a game, then withdrawing emotionally afterward. This significant flaw in his personality was beginning to become a major issue in our marriage. I felt his anger was out of control and made our lives miserable.

At one point in my own frustration, I put a laundry basket over Brian's head when we were playing in the backyard. I playfully threw tennis balls at him so he would get over the fear of balls flying in his direction. Although he thought this was funny, it didn't seem to help in the least. I tried to help Brian see the humor in all the sports hoopla and to keep a perspective on what really mattered, like having fun and being part of a team. He was in it because his friends were involved and not because he expected to play professionally. If there was any consolation to this situation, it was that I saw other fathers behaving as badly as Sam. Brian's best friend, Jimmy, had a father who expressed almost the identical responses at games. This was a pathetic comfort to me. I guess I told myself that at least the fathers were interested in the kids, if somewhat misguided in their expectations. Years later, I've observed that most often the laid-back, mildly supportive fathers somehow produced the most accomplished sports stars.

I had grown up in a family with minimal interest in sports so it was hard for me to understand my husband's zealot-like approach to winning. My brother had been a star football player, yet my father had never bothered to go see his own son play a game. He'd said he worked hard, was too tired and didn't have time for such nonsense. He didn't attend plays or parent-teacher conferences, either. By the time my younger sister ran track, I think my father was retired and went to see her run a few times. Wild horses, however, could not have kept our mother away from our activities.

My twin boys moved on to college and were no longer devoted to competitive sports as other priorities won their interest. They had spent many years with their father yelling from the sidelines. At about age twelve, they stopped playing baseball when they would have spent most of the time bench warming. As soon as they graduated from high school, their interest in playing soccer cooled, then all but evaporated during college years. Although scholarships and college level soccer were Sam's dreams, they didn't materialize for the boys. Eventually, they played recreationally on men's teams or enjoyed spectator sports. As it turned out, Brian sat on the bench during freshman football, and the one time he was on the field during a game, he ran the ball in the wrong direction.

Brian earned his Park City High School track jacket at age 16. Photo taken with Mom on Christmas Day, the last holiday shared with his father in the family home.

Surprisingly, he came into his own with cross country running and track. He ran like the wind and became one of the fastest runners in the state. I was a fast runner in high school, and have to admit, I truly loved watching Brian run with incredible speed, confidence, talent and strategy. Unfortunately, as his illness and complications with medicine began to take over, his abilities waned, and he developed issues with the coach and the team. Then he decided he wouldn't run if his father attended a meet. The day of his last race, I urged Brian to leave the hallway where he was hiding in the high school, hovering on the floor, and run the race he was scheduled to run. When he said he didn't want to, I assured him I hadn't enjoyed childbirth, either. He finally got up and went out to the track but was eliminated for being late. That was the end of his career. Brian dropped out of running completely by his senior year which literally drove his father over the edge with disappointment and disproportionate anger. All possibilities for a scholarship had disintegrated along with the physical disintegration that was going on in Brian's brain.

An insightful letter Brian wrote on this topic follows:

Dear Father,

It's time I spilled my guts. I've feared the truth for so long, as I've always tried to protect everyone. I tried to control myself, and yes, I admit I did lose it more than once, and I did direct that anger towards you alone. But I tried, you see. I never wanted to hurt anyone—I only wanted to help.

I failed, of course. Anyone could see the outcome a long time before it happened. I could not possibly carry the load of my brothers, my mother, and my hate all on my shoulders and still live comfortably. So began the depression, the infamous depression.

When naked anger reveals itself, it's frightening. I had hated a few of your personal traits since the beginning. You never hit me or hurt me physically, but you did emotionally damage me. Those father and son games of catch could not leave an eight- year-old boy unharmed, you know. Just recently I realized why I hated football so much, why it left me feeling so uncomfortable. I hadn't learned to walk when the rule was established that I should never be in the room while my father watched football. That was the rule, no questions asked. I was supposed to leave you alone when it came to fixing car engines and sprinklers. All those father-son experiences—

Fathers and sons should play catch together. My father was the first string pitcher freshman year—and that guy could throw. I never learned to throw right, you know. You bitched me out, screamed, arms wildly flailing in frustration and disgust. You were not proud. No, you were embarrassed of your first son. When you encouraged me, you really discouraged me. You forced me in and then tripped me every step of the way—then you covered up. You were assistant coach, shouting "Jimminy Cricket" from the side-lines. How could I be so ungrateful for all the things you did for me? How could you be so manipulative?

Although there is a bit of truth to almost everything in Brian's note-books, his words are an in-depth mirror of the deterioration going on in his mind. He had unflattering comments to write about friends, teachers, relatives or the world in general. He would fill an entire notebook saying he hated one particular person. After high school, his handwriting seemed to be deteriorating along with his mind, also becoming disorganized and unreadable, just as his life was doing simultaneously. As a teacher, I often see students' handwriting as a window to their mental health. A student might have huge lettering that shrinks to an incredibly miniscule size, depending on the current level of their self-esteem or other complicated issues in their lives.

INEVITABLE DIVORCE

By 1992, our long-term marriage was completely falling apart. We'd moved locally in Park City, remodeled an older house, and suddenly it seemed, a marriage that had survived since 1971 could not be repaired. I think now that it did not fail, but it did expire or maybe I just got tired of gluing it back together. As the children grew older, our common ground and interests had disappeared. I became physically and emotionally starved in our relationship. While my husband's work became all encompassing, valid or not, with more time away from Utah, my world remained around the boys as well as their activities and lives. Despite my love and interest in them, I felt very depressed and suicidal during those years. I spent one day in my closet with a gun, which my husband knew and chose to ignore. Obviously, I was crying out desperately for some attention. Instead, he watched a football game that day and said nothing to me. He often joked in the company of others that supporting me emotionally was a full-time job. In private, he often threatened to "have me put away." I felt continually undervalued, invisible and unloved.

He once gave me an anniversary card that said I would be taken on a trip to Hawaii on the condition that I lost twenty pounds. My weight stayed about the same, but in the years that followed, I made several trips to Hawaii with other friends. One trip, I even managed to take the three boys. A few years after Brian's death, I came across some undeveloped film in the garage, and quickly had those pictures developed. I was shaking with disbelief when I saw Brian's sixteen-year-old face staring back at me. What a gift it was to find that old film and reaffirm those wonderful memories we had made in Hawaii. I can even recall being worried at the time that Brian slept so much while Cody and Dillon, age twelve, were busily checking out the girls on the beach. There were so many signs that I simply explained away.

After a continually disappointing career in real estate sales, during which I lacked the competitive ruthlessness to succeed, I worked part time in a real estate office with little interest in conquering the market and moving into the big time. As our resort town was growing by megabounds, more deals incorporated drugs, sex, power or whatever was marketable. I realize now how angry my husband was that I was not competitive enough to establish a solid money-based real estate career. It was a great job for a piranha, but I realistically considered myself to be a guppy. I had been his disappointing project that had failed to live up to his expectations, just as Brian was, too.

Eventually, Sam didn't have to look far to discover a female geologist that he worked with and one with whom he could share his challenging career. In retaliation, stubbornness and following my adventuresome spirit, I began spending more time in Los Angeles, and following my interest in screenwriting. I would have been willing to compromise and work things out in the marriage, forever the peacemaker, but he hungered for his new life back East. Unfortunately, all that the controversy accomplished was an anger-filled relationship and a long, drawn out, expensive divorce. The attorneys and the court bought into this tortuous process, expressing little concern for the pain that the family was put through in custody issues, selling our home and emotional and financial upheaval. After three years of harassment and finding letters from attorneys in the mail almost everyday, I finally just wanted it over at all costs. I would give up everything except joint custody.

When I initially told the boys there would be a divorce, Cody and Dillon, age 12, shrugged and went out to play. At least half of their friends' parents were divorced in this ski town environment. In my observation, people seemed to move to the idyllic town of Park City hoping to leave their problems back in L. A. or from wherever they had sprung. The concentration of wealth and undiluted *type A* personalities often resulted in continuing problems, especially in not having their expectations realized. According to an old survey I'd read in *Ski Magazine*, divorce rates were higher in a resort town than the national average at that time.

Cody expressed that at least his father would still be around, unlike another child's father who had died. He also said he was tired of our fighting. I was surprised since I had tried so hard to keep any arguments out of the boys' hearing. Unfortunately, Cody's room was located closest to ours. Sam and I had often driven in the car for a discussion, parked a few blocks away and continued arguing out our frustrations. The looks on our faces when we returned must have said everything that words hadn't. Everyday, I am still haunted, not only by my own parental mistakes, but also by the heartbreak and pain that my students suffer as their parents divorce and the children end up blaming themselves.

THANKSGIVING 1993

I spent the morning crying. For the first time since our marriage in 1971, there would be no Thanksgiving dinner at our house. In August, the day after our twenty-third anniversary, my husband had told me he'd found someone else and had soon moved out of our family home. Incredibly, he was gone the next major holiday, Thanksgiving, as if that were normal procedure. Without apology, he was suddenly expected for dinner at another family's home back East where he had apparently been visiting quite often during the past year. His trade of campsite and allegiance felt to us as if it had occurred overnight.

I remember this moment clearly, standing in Brian's room. It was a disorganized mess, as always. He was sixteen, lanky and muscular, with sharply handsome features and a thatch of straw-colored hair. He'd dressed in his ski suit and insisted he was going skiing. I kept asking him if he would ride with me to the country to visit friends. No, he wanted to ski, he'd said. I left for a few hours to find my way from Park City to Woodland, a remote little hamlet outside our resort town. I wasn't going to stay for dinner, just a visit.

The sun was so bright on the snow that my eyes burned from all the crying. With no make-up and my long hair out of control, I resembled the terrible expression of "death warmed over." Incredibly, this was the day I met my present husband. Jim was a slender giant of a man, six foot eight. He was quiet and shy, playing with the dogs in the yard. When he asked if I wanted to ride a four-wheeler, I thought he was joking. I think I might have laughed aloud at the absurdity of it all.

I returned home and found Brian stretched out asleep on his bed, his feet on the floor, still dressed in his ski suit. At first I thought he was unconscious. It was too warm to be sleeping in a ski suit, especially in the middle of the afternoon. When I awakened him, he said he'd been too tired to ski. That was the first incident of unusually strange behavior that made me wonder if something was wrong with him.

Strangely, Brian, just turning 16, seemed relieved at the news of the divorce and said he hoped we would both finally be happy. He and I drove up to Guardsman's Pass above Park City and took a long hike. He seemed philosophical and accepting, seemingly unconcerned that this thing could take on a mean, vindictive life of its own. I had actually solicited the help of a mediator the first year. I realized later, the attorney acted in his own interests, taking money from both of us and setting us up in adversarial positions from the get go. The first attorney even lied to me about acquiring a restraining order against my husband but failed to do so. This act alone left me vulnerable to vicious verbal and potentially dangerous physical attacks.

I ended up having three different attorneys, losing our home, moving with the boys nine times in three years, and often finding myself unemployed, homeless and lacking insurance. My previously excellent health deteriorated with panic attacks, asthma, arthritis, pneumonia, high blood pressure and post traumatic stress syndrome.

During the struggle of the divorce, I wrote with some insight into my self-absorbed situation. I had maintained a romance with the ocean for some years and often thought with a great sense of melancholy and depression that I would die there. I regret terribly that I shared that idea of drowning with Brian. During the years of separation and delayed divorce, I made several trips to Los Angeles, writing screenplays as a writer from Utah and struggling with marketing as an L.A. outsider. I had met such celebrities as Sid Luft, Judy Garland's former husband, Marlon Brando, Faye Dunaway, Kate Jackson, David Hasselhoff as well as many others through the Sundance Film Festival. There was just enough encouragement to keep my interest in screenwriting, similar to priming slot machines in Vegas. Little did I realize, this hectic commuting between my two lives was the calm before the hurricane.

OCEANSIDE, CALIFORNIA – FEBRUARY, 1995 - REFLECTIONS

I was doing peanut butter when everyone else was doing coke. Today the road is fifty feet from the balcony and the sand and sea just beyond. For February, it is mild, sunny, 65 degrees with gentle breezes, a far cry from the freezing cold of Utah winter. Wearing shorts, having a glass of wine, my life is a far away, forgotten reflection of reality/fantasy.

All the trips west now meld into one blurred memory of times and friends that make me wistful and melancholy for what might have been. The people's faces fade just as the tide leaves with fresh unmarked sand, no longer printed with their footsteps and voices on my memory. My life has reached a different stage of goals and resolutions that were hardly a part of the picture then. Now there are changes in goals to achieve and decisions to make. I've reached some sort of awkward balance in the reality of my present life from what I once dreamed would be real.

Maybe this is what we all seek—finding that balance between what is, what should have been, and what can never be again. I'm moved by the mood of my companion Jim and what a contrast he is from the piranha people of my past dealings who were only out for their own selfish purposes. The peacefulness of the ocean overwhelms my senses, both with its strength and power, yet brings soothing inner comfort to my worn psyche.

The longings wash over me for the visits to Malibu, Topanga, Beverly Hills and all that brought me to this point. Part of me has denied the existence of those times, the love I felt for my freedom after years of being emotionally imprisoned. However, the overpowering need to exist with my children takes control over my desire to be free. It is enough to change the situation where another controlled my every move and questioned all my motives. That alone gives me a great sense of well being that all will be right in my world soon enough. Never again would I endure such subtle passivity, anger, aggression, tyranny as I have for these two decades.

I will hope that the boys understand in the long run it is much better to be true to one's self and own the responsibility to grow and be who you are rather than stifled in some cocoon. My only regret is the long time necessary to achieve this acceptance and understanding of myself. Now I will grow and become who I should have been so long ago—then a young girl in search of her own fulfillment, not side-tracked by someone else's career. The boys are definitely the only assets I'd achieved—not the materialism we had acquired. I look forward to a future of my own making by choosing to succeed without fear or force.

Jim is all that I could hope for in a man who is at peace with himself and secure with who he is, unaware of his influence on my soul. He has unwittingly replaced my fears for the future with peace of mind. I can now accept things I cannot change and have no control to do so. For all my struggles, I have yet to achieve this acceptance of who I am, guiltless of how others perceive me or themselves. How could I have maintained such an empty shell of a marriage for so many years? Maybe that is the one thought that overwhelms me with its incredibility. How could

I have lost myself for someone who was so thankless and oblivious? In the end, I have only the trite excuse that I stayed in the marriage, rather than face raising the children alone without a father.

A silver sunset. Not orange. It is appropriate that it is a day sparkled by the sun, not glamorized by red lighting.

DISINTEGRATION

Along with all the complications of the three-year struggle to divorce, Brian began falling apart during that time, too. Once when I called from L. A., Brian, at age fourteen, said his father had left on an overnight business trip to Las Vegas. Brian insisted there was nothing to eat in the house except canned soup. Not only did he sound depressed, he sounded overwhelmed with the responsibility of taking care of his ten-year-old brothers. I was furious that Sam had left them without even telling me. Blaming myself, too, I immediately headed for home, resolute to once again put the pieces of our family life back together. As a further disconnect, I recall an earlier time when their father sent them to me in L. A. with a total of twenty dollars, hardly covering their lunch. Our family bond had disintegrated to the point that I finally gave up writing screenplays, returned home and became the anchor while their father moved away to Virginia to live with his new imaginary family.

SENIOR YEAR, 1996

With the beginning of his senior year near, I finally realized I couldn't handle Brian any longer. I was shocked when he physically threw me down in the front yard and stood over me, yelling obscenities. It happened during the middle of the day in the bright sunshine in front of any neighbor who cared to look. In some way, I was terrified because the behavior was so random and flagrant. What might happen to me or the twins when there were no witnesses? In the shock of the moment, it never occurred to me to call the police. My parents in Texas offered to try to help Brian by removing him from ill-chosen associates and family conflicts. Brian moved to Texas and began his senior year in high school there the fall of 1995.

Within two weeks, he begged to return to Utah and his friends. Since I didn't think my parents could really handle the situation, either, I arranged for him to fly to Las Vegas where I picked him up by car. I remember him arriving with several suitcases, his guitar and a floppy hat, in addition to wearing a big grin. He promised he would stay out of trouble, go to school, etc. One of the biggest concerns he'd expressed was that while he was in Texas, he worried each day he'd return from school and find Grandpa had died.

Thus, began the cycle of moving from one place to another as our finances crumbled. Each time we moved, Brian seemed to have a more serious type of breakdown. Being dislocated was the worst effect on his illness that happened to him over and over during the next few years. Just after his return from Texas, in October of his senior year, I finally moved out of the home we'd shared with his dad and surrendered the $2,400 per month payments I could not afford but was under court order to pay. Before our separation, we had struggled on $5,000 income per month to make ends meet for five people when our family was still intact. Our income was below average compared to the surrounding friends and neighbors whose yearly salary in this resort town was several hundred thousand dollars. Although this fact never particularly bothered me, it was very distressing to my husband to try to keep up with everyone else while employed by the government. He always dreamed of owning a boat, or at least a much nicer car or home. While I was unpacking our things in the move to Park City, he was already talking about his next promotion and move to Washington, D.C. Typical of a child of an alcoholic, he was always living in the future in his own fantasy/escape world. This attitude helped him to detach completely from our financial hardships as he left Park City and moved on to his long sought after life in D.C. He bought a house in Virginia as an investment while he continued to live with his beloved and her two daughters. Ironically, he kept a condo in Park City that he rarely visited in order to "maintain his lifestyle."

According to the wisdom of the Utah court system, it would be necessary for me to maintain a home and existence for four people on $2,500 a month in a high income, high rent ski area with a home mortgage of $2,400. The announcement of the Winter Olympics 2002 instantly aided the skyrocketing rental costs from $600 per month for an average home to $1,500. Working at various jobs for $8 an hour was never going to make up the difference in our lost income. As my attorney pointed out, I was marketing a twenty-five-year-old liberal arts degree I'd barely used. For a few months that fall, I worked standing on my feet in a grocery bakery, came home, put my feet up and cried. By March, I had to give up our first rental house. My father generously paid to have our belongings moved to Texas although he visibly choked at the expensive price tag. As I was leaving Park City and trying to fill my prescriptions, I learned that I no longer had any insurance coverage. I cried every mile between Utah and East Texas. The worst part was leaving Brian to live with a friend those last months of his senior year. Thank God Evelyn was so generous in opening her home to Brian those few months.

When we settled in a $600 rental house near my parents, my now ex-husband requested the court to lower payments to us because of our reduced expenses, again making our survival further impossible. I remember the twins and I sitting in my hometown living room waiting solemnly for the mail and a check that meant we could buy food. We often ate dinner at my parents' house where the boys drank milk and ate meat since we couldn't even afford the basics. Finally, while waiting for the house in Park City to sell, I was faced with the humiliating task of a bankruptcy in order to start over financially. My parents cried when I told them. Having lived through The Great Depression, my hardships couldn't have been worse news for them. For the most part, my extended family treated my financial problems as the equivalent of shameful character flaws and criminal behavior.

Ironically, this perception of self-inflicted financial ruin is similar to the social attitude that corresponds to the stigma of mental illness. I've often wondered if those who sit in judgment really believe people caught in these life-destroying situations willingly desire or choose to be homeless, ill or unemployed. American society is ignorant and arrogant to believe those lives aren't full of tortuous pain, and often, mental illness.

As an example, although my brother had a job with his company advertised in the local newspaper and a larger car for sale, he never once offered any help. I earned $40 a day substitute teaching and that was the most dependable job I could find in my small hometown. Even though I'd grown up in East Texas, it didn't help that I'd moved from Utah, which implied I had to be Mormon in the minds of these good East Texas Baptists. Amusing, too, was the necessity of driving my compact car in which the boys had to fold up their growing 6'4" frames.

The boys were unhappy and socially cut off in a very different, primarily redneck culture. They got off the school bus and hid in their rooms, hardly speaking to me or to anyone else. When the three of us returned to Park City for graduation, courtesy of tickets provided by Delta pilots through friends' families, the twins begged never to leave again. They were reunited with their band to play for their eighth grade graduation and to attend Brian's high school graduation. For six weeks, we managed, without a car or a home, to live in Park City through the unlimited kindness and generosity of friends.

Upon graduation, Brian went to live in an old hotel which was basically a half-way house on Main St. He became very disconnected from us during this time. His facial responses had shut down, called *flat affect*, to the point he hardly responded to anything we said to him. One day when I told him someone we knew had died, he laughed as if it were a joke. Now I realize this detachment is an obvious symptom of *schizophrenia*, a complex and serious mental illness. According to *Surviving Schizophrenia* by E. Fuller Torrey, indications include catatonic symptoms, paranoid symptoms, the presence of depression, the predominance of "negative symptoms, such as flattening of emotions, poverty of thoughts, apathy and social withdrawal, obsessive compulsive symptoms and extreme confusion." At that time, I assumed Brian was doing drugs, but he never admitted to the drugs or to his illness. There were many signs that we completely missed or misinterpreted from our own lack of medical knowledge or understanding of *duel diagnosis*. Now I realize he was self-medicating for his mental disease, and he was addicted to drugs in order to feel more "normal" in the depths of his illness.

By July, I returned to Texas to sell many of our belongings and pack the rest in storage. I had garage sales that included selling my white leather living room set and antique dining room furniture, my twenty-three year old wedding gown and family bible. Nothing of sentimental value seemed to matter any more. I drove back to Utah in August and lived in a donated condo, thanks to Kathy, with the boys and our dog for a month while we waited on the list for low-income housing. The boys willingly agreed to live in a box near their friends rather than live in the house in Texas.

When I returned to Park City, I recall that my little sheltie, Willow, ran up to Brian on the street. My son just stared at her and at me as if we were strangers. He was long-haired, barefooted, dressed in ragged clothes and almost unrecognizable. His "Oh, hi, Mom," sounded as if we'd seen each other that morning rather than months before. At this point, I realized that Brian was becoming more distanced emotionally than ever. He rarely interacted with me, his brothers or even the beloved Willow.

I cried when I had to give away the dog in order to live in low-income housing. It seemed that I had given up everything already. Willow was a total nuisance, but she was unconditionally loving and a great comfort to all of us. I had left my cat of thirteen years, Sugar, in Texas with my parents, and she eventually ran away. It seemed I had no control of hanging on to the things, animals or people that I loved.

LOW INCOME HOUSING

By September, Jim Baker, who later became my husband, flew with me to Texas and met my parents. We loaded up the storage items and drove the rental truck back to Utah. Although my parents, who were elderly and needed help, said I should go take care of the boys and get on with my life, I felt terribly guilty leaving them. Still, I couldn't find a decent job in Texas and without extra income, I would have to give the kids over to their father who now lived in Virginia. That one factor in the divorce was my main purpose in fighting all along. The boys had refused to move to Virginia and my only concern was their happiness with whatever stability I could provide. If I could not support them, they would have to go live with their father, whether they wanted to or not. Sam told me viciously on the phone one night that he would destroy me "emotionally and financially." He was very thorough in his revenge. My "settlement" after 23 years of marriage was $10,000 with my legal fees alone totaling $16,000. My leaving the family home with the $2,400 payments meant those were later deducted from my share. In other words, I was charged with double "rent" for our housing.

Finally, I found an office job that was still only $8 an hour but at least included benefits in 90 days and a chair so I didn't have to stand for eight hours as I had at the bakery. In September, Jim helped us move to the fourth floor of newly-built low income housing, and I was grateful to finally have a roof over our heads in Park City. Our rent was only $611 a month so we could actually make ends meet for the first time since Sam left. Our yearly income for four people was $18,000 which was less than the national poverty level. One day in January when I stayed home with pneumonia, Sam came to the door with a container of soup. He was tan from his trip to Aruba and stopped by to see the boys on his return to Virginia. I remember blood pouring from my nose because of a reaction from high blood pressure and over the counter medications. I still lacked insurance and money for a doctor. Sam was argumentative and insisted his trip to Aruba "hadn't cost him a nickel." A good friend had told me the best revenge was to be happy. I was trying despite all odds.

UNIVERSITY OF UTAH, 1996

Brian was enrolled at the University of Utah as a freshman that year. Reviewing his grades, which I finally wrestled from the registrar following his death, was insightful. His grades indicated he had started the year well in the fall but they had declined to nothing by the end of the year.

At one point, I had to persuade Brian to dress in a white shirt and tie as I accompanied him to court for possession of marijuana. He had met a friend at a park above the university area to share some weed, and the friend's car was impounded. Brian's father had paid an attorney to defend him as this was his first offense, and he would have no record. The only earlier run-in with the law was a very slight speeding ticket in high school to which Brian had reacted angrily and spoken harshly with the judge. I remember being surprised by Brian's rebellious attitude despite his obvious guilt. I was grateful the judge did not put Brian in jail for his perplexing outburst.

LIVING IN OBLIVION

By the end of his freshman year in college, Brian crowded into our tiny Park City apartment, slept on the sofa and began working for a local paint store. He drove vans and delivered paint all over the Salt Lake Valley. I had acquired a telecommuting job with a magazine company in Denver and went there to learn the ropes for a month. The younger boys had gone to Virginia to visit their father, and Brian was living alone in the apartment. Jim checked on him and reported the place was a huge disorganized mess. Piles of dishes sat with food stuck on them and clothes were strewn everywhere. Fortunately, Jim persuaded him to clean up the mess before I returned home.

One night Brian called me in Denver and said he was quitting the paint store job. He said the other employees made fun of him and rolled huge cans of paint at him. He said he was going camping in the High Uinta Mountains for three weeks and would call me when he returned. I was frightened for him, sensing that he planned to commit suicide and would never return from the mountains. His world was methodically falling apart, and I was confined to the office in Denver. I was relieved to learn Brian had returned to the apartment after camping for only three days, having forgotten bug spray and matches.

When I returned from Denver, I decided we would take on renting a house again, so Brian and Jim helped me move out of the tiny apartment to a large older house in Park City. This was a leap of faith that the magazine job would work out well, plus my income now exceeded the requirements for assisted housing. After the move, Brian was distressed and difficult to live with, no longer working but staying out all night and sleeping all day. He was not planning to return to college and seemed aimless and depressed. Once when his father visited, I asked him to wait while I awakened Brian, and then I practically dragged him out to the car. An hour later, Sam dropped him off, checked his watch and sped away for the airport. His excuse for every departure was "I have a plane to catch." While refusing to take parental responsibility in helping with Brian's condition, Sam left me with the continual burden of desperately searching for resources and help of any kind. I was becoming more and more frustrated in trying to get Brian motivated or to at least get some outside help for him. Whatever was wrong with him, I knew he could not continue living in such a state of depression that influenced all of us.

His friends were starting to disappear out of his life. Old high school buddies had moved on to prestigious universities, sorority girls and plans for the future. Most of the ambitious ones no longer returned his phone calls which really frustrated him. The days he shared intellectual pursuits such as academic decathlon and filmmaking had long passed. He was lucky to have a few more socially available friends who worked in computer technology without the advantage of a college education. However, some of these friends habitually attended drug parties and raves in Salt Lake City and provided a continual source of drugs. I worried about everything Brian was doing for recreation, but there was no way to control him by withholding something he wanted or having him committed to a contract as friends and professionals suggested. I was not dealing with someone who could be reasoned with, not a normal wayward child who would outgrow this stage. My frustration was increasing this year while I worked for the magazine at home and became acutely aware of Brian's party and sleep cycle schedule.

Cody and Dillon returned from Virginia in July to find we'd moved out of the tiny apartment to the larger house. I had wanted to surprise the twins, and they were ecstatic to be back in their old neighborhood near school and friends. Often I would be in the office doing a magazine phone interview when they would come in from school full of noise and excitement. Dillon told me later that this was his happiest year of school, and there was so much more food since I had a better job. They were so grateful to be in their own home and that year they grew from skinny kids to tall, muscled young men.

*Jim took our photo on a camping trip to Trial Lake
in the High Uintas of Utah. Brian slept most of the time.*

It was a good year for me and for Jim, too. He became more and more a part of the family, spending time fishing and camping with the boys. I loved that he came over, cooked and even provided dinner in addition to fixing or painting everything that needed maintenance. Initially, he could not believe that a husband and father would leave his family in such conditions. He looked at the heater's clogged air filter in disbelief, knowing that it provided a likely firetrap located directly next to the laundry. The ceiling leaked, the fireplace smoked, and the dishwasher overflowed but Jim took it all in stride. He set a great example to the boys by whistling rather than ranting through the entire formidable mess.

REALITY CHECK

Unfortunately, at Christmas, I was abruptly fired from my magazine job and felt devastated over the loss. The company decided they were cutting back, regardless that it was the holiday season. I'd already bought plane tickets to Texas so that Cody and Dillon could visit their grandparents. Sam then furiously claimed it was his turn to have them in Virginia for Christmas so they ended up visiting for twenty-four hours in Texas before being shipped on to Virginia. That was the last time they saw their grandfather.

On the flight home from Dallas, just over Salt Lake City, I had the strangest experience that someone was telling me to stay with Jim even if it meant until his death. It was an overwhelming feeling that God or others were trying to communicate with me. It was that strange whisper-in-the-ear experience I'd known a few other times. Jim was entrenched in alcoholism, and we were very co-dependent, I realized. He needed me as much as I needed him, yet I was frustrated with his continued drinking. My doctor had told me to get rid of him, that he would never quit. I'd even visited a co-dependency group to try to understand why I had been labeled as "over-mothering" my son who was on drugs and why I had attracted a man who was an alcoholic.

A few weeks later on a bright Sunday afternoon, Jim left several phone messages that he was in his truck at an isolated frozen lake. He sounded quite drunk, and I worried that most likely he had a gun with him. He was obviously distressed, and I felt both sympathy and anger that he couldn't get his life together. Finally, I reached a fishing buddy of his, Frank, and asked him to call Jim's cell phone and talk him into coming back to town. Frank succeeded in getting Jim to drive home. Amazingly, and through the grace of God, Jim quit drinking after that incident. It was my birthday and he gave me the most precious gift of his life through sobriety and the touch of God on his soul. A few years later on my fiftieth birthday, he gave up smoking, too.

Our lives changed from that point forward. Jim gave up on a failed business partnership that had resulted in his increased drinking and the two of us, both unemployed, took a trip to Hawaii on savings Jim had squirreled away. We drank non-alcoholic fruit drinks, and he found himself surrounded by a world of beauty that had never existed in his alcohol-induced fog. Although I had cared very much for Jim, I had never before looked at him as a potential mate and husband. Our relationship had grown out of friendship, mutual support, acceptance and respect.

I have to admit that when I first met Jim, I was so despondent, I was more interested in the fact that he had guns as well as alcohol. With my increasingly painful divorce, I sometimes thought there must be a way out of the pain. I was so distressed, I would fantasize eliminating myself from the picture, and the boys would still have their father, but the fighting would be over. Although I probably drank more wine than I should have during this time of depression, I never reached the point of following through on a suicide attempt. Despite all my problems, the boys mattered more to me than anything else and gave me purpose in living. I found that Jim was becoming the friend and support system I needed to get through the worst of times. He also had the wisdom to get rid of his guns, probably because of me as well as Brian.

PROGRESSIVE BRAIN DISEASE

During this time, I saw little of Brian as he wandered from living with the few friends he still had. It's amazing to me now to realize how much these friends took care of Brian. He rarely paid rent or bought food. If he had any money from a temporary job, he quickly spent it by buying breakfast for homeless people in the street. His father had developed an attitude that if Brian would "prove" to him that he could work for a year, then he would again pay tuition to send him back to college. Brian was incapable of staying with a job more than temporarily, usually only a few days. Most likely, he couldn't have handled college, either, without taking medication. After the paint store job, he remained with a printing company for a few weeks as a delivery driver. Construction, detours and congested traffic were becoming the norm in Salt Lake City with the coming of the Olympics 2002. One day he told me the traffic drove him crazy, so he pulled the truck off the road and took a two-hour nap. His mental abilities were breaking down and his resilience was becoming diminished as he spent more time losing focus and wandering the streets.

Brian still seemed somewhat in control at age 20,
despite dropping out of college. He drove Grandpa's old '67
Chevy pickup that I had driven in high school.

Although he collected job applications, he rarely filled them out. If he worked a few days, he often did not return to pick up his pay. When he died, his papers included over thirty blank job application forms. He'd worn out the soles of his shoes from all his days of walking aimlessly. One time in an angry fit, Brian said his father could never have lived even one week on the streets. This was probably true as his father has maintained the same job with benefits and security since he was twenty-three years old. Sam continually ridiculed the two of us for our inability to find substantial employment.

Off and on, Brian would come home to live with me and the boys for a while, rest and eat well. He promised not to argue with his brothers, but the situation was always temporary. With the progressive deterioration going on in his brain, he'd get on a tangent of wanting them to try different drugs, then I felt compelled to throw him out once again. This continuing "tough love" scenario tore my heart out. I would curl up on my bed, feeling defeated, scared and hopeless. I thought I was losing my mind and no matter where I turned, there seemed to be no answers and no help. The general consensus with several doctors had been to leave him alone, let him grow up and stop "over-mothering" him. Even a doctor friend who had attended eighteen years of college told me quite angrily that Brian didn't want or need me interfering in his life.

I'd driven Brian to Ogden, Utah to a specialist who confided in Brian that he, too, had enjoyed smoking weed and shifting from one job to another when he was young. I suppose he was trying to get Brian to trust him, but this good ol' boy script infuriated me. The doctor didn't help him in the least, prescribing Paxil for social anxiety when Brian probably needed lithium. It didn't seem to matter which medicine was prescribed, at any rate. After a few weeks of nauseous side effects, Brian would inevitably quit taking the medicine. Once in a while, he'd seem fairly optimistic that the new prescription was working. I recall an incident where Brian went to southern Utah with friends and had forgotten his meds. He tried to get them refilled at the pharmacy but couldn't persuade them to help him. Of course, he had terrible headaches, and his friends were less than sympathetic, not understanding the seriousness of his illness.

Since I'd lost my magazine job at Christmas, the following spring we moved once more to a small condo that was half the cost of the house rent. I particularly remember while we were moving, Brian had a headache and went to lie on the grass. Jim was carrying a king-sized mattress, and I could not believe Brian just walked away from helping him. I realize now how much pain and suffering Brian had to be experiencing to become so detached from us.

I had become a curator at an art center and was feeling a great deal of pressure to produce exhibits and education classes. Much to my embarrassment, Brian often showed up at my office, demanding money and starting arguments with me. The day of my first children's exhibit, the police called ten times. They'd found Brian's old '67 Chevy truck involved in a burglary in Salt Lake City the evening before. The young men were caught in the act by the owner but managed to escape. The police asked me such questions as where Brian lived and whether he had cut his hair or shaved off his beard recently.

Finally, feeling harassed and hoping to clear him, I gave the police the address of the apartment where he'd been living with his high school friend near the university. Initially, we'd been relieved he had an apartment and helped furnish it and bought food for him. Later, we noticed the chest of drawers sat in the same center spot in his bedroom the day we brought it and the day we moved it to storage. The drawers remained empty, and the floor was covered with clothing. At some point, Sam stopped financing Brian's rent, and he could not make enough money on his own. He'd run out of rent money and had begged his brothers to buy the old truck from him some months earlier that winter. They were both working in restaurants, nights and weekends, making hard won money. I would not have let them buy the truck from Brian under any circumstances. It was originally my father's, and one I had driven in high school. My father had given it to my husband who, despite the divorce decree, still held the title and refused to hand it over to me or to Brian. The truck was symbolic of the conflict between all of us. Much later, we sold that truck after Brian died and just before my father died. The money was split between the twins.

The police interrogated Brian for six hours to no avail. According to the police, his story was that he was smoking weed with some guys at a park in Salt Lake City. He lost the keys to the truck and walked home to the apartment. He had no knowledge of how those guys got the keys, took his truck without permission and proceeded to get involved in a burglary. The owner had driven up to his house and caught them in the act of looting his garage. They scattered before they could be identified. The final call from the detective indicated his frustration that he knew something was going on with Brian but could not pinpoint what was wrong. I have felt very guilty that if I had not told the police where he was, then he would not have lost his apartment. The police breaking in was the last straw for the room- mate to whom Brian still owed overdue rent. Brian held no grudge about my telling the police his address as he knew he wasn't guilty. Any follow up questions I asked of his friends confirmed that they believed Brian was innocent.

CRIMINAL JUSTICE SYSTEM

I've learned that often the only way for someone like Brian to get help for mental illness is through the criminal justice system. By going through the back door in the system, the police sometimes recognize that an individual needs medication more than he needs to be imprisoned. I've often heard the statistic quoted that half the people in prisons need medication for mental illness, but they are not getting the help they need. Recently, I asked a Houston judge who responded she believed *all prisoners had some type of mental illness*. Being an inmate costs the government, i.e., taxpayers, a great deal more ($50,000 per year vs. $5,000) than helping the mentally ill receive medication and become productive members of society. The legal system is slowly catching up to the fact that incarceration doesn't work, especially with the rehabilitation of celebrity addiction cases that are played out in the news. Even with available finances and the support of Hollywood, actors who seem blessed with so many gifts, continue to land back in jail. How much harder it must be for the average inmate to receive proper medication, counseling and recovery methods without support.

After the incident over Brian's truck burglary, I was more aware that his mental health was going downhill fast that summer. My office was on Main Street, and he would show up with wild accusations and out of control behavior. The policy that university personnel at the psychiatric hospital adhered to held that Brian had to make his own appointment. He refused any help in making the appointment. I have never understood the logic in expecting a mentally ill person who does not believe they are ill to seek medical help on their own. I decided the university ruling was absurd.

I called the Park City police following one confrontation that summer and explained my concerns. I was very worried that if he had one of his fits and the police were called, they might shoot him in confusion over his behavior. Although I didn't consider him usually violent or "a threat to himself or society," I was becoming less sure of his angry rages. Detective Mary Ford with the Park City Police Department said that the next time he had a public outburst, I should call the police and report Brian for disturbing the peace. According to her experience and the fact that she had a mentally ill brother, she expressed that she was almost certain Brian was *schizophrenic*. However, unless the police had been given a reason to pick him up, they could not hold him for seventy-two hours in order to analyze his condition.

I felt both shocked and relieved to hear there was an identifiable reason for his extreme behavior. I knew exactly nothing about the symptoms, causes or long term picture of schizophrenia. Immediately, I called his father in Virginia to tell him what I'd learned. His response, which I remember perfectly was, "That's your own paranoia. There's nothing wrong with Brian. How could the police tell you on the phone he might have schizophrenia without even seeing him?" Despite his insistent denial, I began to think there was a mental disease that had attacked my son's brain and had left him devastated. There had to be an answer for the change in personality that was stealing our son's life. He had been a consistently loving, affectionate, productive, happy individual in earlier years. I no longer recognized my boy as the same person except for occasional glimpses of his old self. Those glimpses came when he'd been self-medicating with alcohol or drugs. Once when he'd been drinking, he came in during the wee hours, singing Irish lullabies. We talked for an hour, and oddly, despite the alcohol, he seemed more coherent and normal than usual.

Brian moved back to the old hotel on Main St. in Park City and incredibly, got thrown out within a few weeks. The hotel was essentially a halfway house for people who were struggling to get on their feet. When the landlady, who was kind and generous beyond belief, found hundreds of burned matches and several spoons in his room, she couldn't take the chance he might burn down the old hotel. Every time Jim and I stopped by to see him and try to persuade him to eat a meal, he was in some stage of sleep, always like he was drugged.

PARANOIA

Brian worked for a Mexican restaurant at that time and was convinced he'd overheard a conversation about a murder. I recall being with Brian in the grocery store when he told me there were people out to kill him because he knew about a murder he'd overheard on a phone call in which someone was speaking Spanish. When I asked what in the world he was talking about, he shushed me, furious that small children on the next aisle would hear us and report back to the murderers. How I could have not known he was insane, I don't know. Having never taken drugs myself, I had no idea what was "normal" in the strange fantasy world where he lived.

He spent that summer doing more drugs, losing weight and fading in and out of our lives. Part of the time, he lived in a flop house in Salt Lake City with someone named Buddy who appeared to me to be almost toothless, mean and scary. One morning, as I was leaving for work, there was another rough looking kid on our doorstep. He'd spent the night talking to Brian in a coffee shop and aggressively threatened me if I didn't help Brian. I was ready to call the police to get rid of him, but he wandered away. For the first time, I was really becoming afraid of the strangers Brian picked up and brought to our home. These were no longer kids he'd known since childhood such as Boy Scouts or exemplary students who had aspirations to become doctors and lawyers. These were people I'd avoid on the street, who might look armed or dangerous for whatever reasons. The fear wasn't only for myself but for the influence on the twins who were still in high school.

I confronted Sam when he came by the condo, and out of pure desperation, I was crying as I once again forced Brian and all his belongings in the car. I remember being hysterical, thinking that his father could at least take care of one of the boys, that I was out of resources and felt the rest of our family was endangered by this situation. An hour later, Sam returned, methodically, with no sign of emotion, dropped off Brian and his things, checked his watch and drove off to the airport. As sick as I am to admit it, I threw Brian out with a tent and some food, telling him he could live in the woods, that I couldn't have him affecting his brothers and driving us all crazy. I was so fed up, I had developed the defense that I was not required by law to live with a twenty-year old drug addict.

After three days, he returned in much worse shape, dirty, angry and hungry. He went ballistic about his wisdom teeth needing to be removed, and that I had never taken care of him properly. Feeling guilty, I did make arrangements for his dental work. Then I realized quite naively, as he spoke to the dentist in depth, that I had been manipulated again and that Brian was overly interested in the drugs that would be used. I put him to bed in my room after the surgery and watched over him for twenty-four hours while he remained in a sound sleep. I have never known anyone who slept a solid day without moving after having wisdom teeth removed. He seemed to be lost beyond my reach with the drugs they'd given him.

My beautiful, brilliant child was deteriorating before my eyes. I knew with certainty my dreams of his going to law school, getting married or having a child's tricycle in his driveway would never materialize. He'd gone from academic decathlon to a homeless addict living in the streets. My instincts told me there had to be something really wrong with him, more than the drugs that kept him in his other world. Unlike the advice I had gotten from friends and doctors, Brian was not going to "outgrow" this.

UTAH TO TEXAS TO VIRGINIA TO UTAH

I sat down and wrote a letter to my family begging for their help. My parents insisted they wanted Brian to come to Texas and that my brother, who had challenged the system while growing up, would also be able to help with him. It was August when I took Brian's picture with his face thin and his eyes darkly shadowed. I reluctantly sent him on a plane to Albuquerque, New Mexico. He wanted to visit his old friend Jimmy and then promised to go on to Texas. Since Jimmy's mother and I were close friends, I hoped this would be a good plan. And, yes, I just wanted him to go anywhere and get straightened out to return to being the person he had been.

He was in New Mexico a few days when my friend called and said Brian should travel on to Texas. The problem was that her son Jimmy was trying to settle into college in Albuquerque and needed to avoid distractions. Understandably, she felt Brian was hardly a good influence in that direction. Some of his writings that I read later indicated he tried a variety of drugs on this trip. Ironically, Jimmy did not continue with college but later found himself on a different path with the arts, travel, meditation and living on a reservation among Native Americans.

Brian managed to survive about two weeks in Texas before my brother had had his fill and abruptly put Brian on a bus without even a suitcase and sent him on to his father in Virginia. I got a panicked call from Brian in Memphis. He was apparently having a psychological breakdown, extreme paranoia, delusions and probably hearing voices. He was convinced someone on the bus was trying to kill him, that a small boy and a policeman in Memphis knew him by name. I asked Brian if he trusted me, and he said he did. I told him to calm down, that I loved him and begged him to please get on the bus to Virginia.

Unfortunately, much later, I learned that Memphis has one of the best police departments for recognizing mental illness and getting help for people in Brian's condition. He had not committed any crime and still was not meeting the criteria of "a threat to himself or society." Even if I had called the police, I doubt they would have been able to apprehend him. I wish I had called them, though.

He did go on to Virginia and stayed at his father's house for a short time. Since Sam was either at work or his girlfriend's house, Brian primarily remained alone behind locked doors. He began calling me, asking for a gun to protect himself from the people on the street who were trying to kill him. He sounded terrified and so alone. Although I worried about him constantly, I was also relieved that now he was under his father's supervision, and the financial and medical resources were available to provide better care for him.

In his isolation, Brian reached out to the one source that would accept him – television. He became obsessed with the singer, Sheryl Crow, and talked about her music constantly. He was convinced his "band" would get back together and be able to play for Sheryl Crow. Sometimes he spoke of marrying her.

From a notebook he wrote during his time in Virginia:

Dear Sheryl,
I am a baffled piece of cowardice, but I wish my band to rise to fame and glory, in spite of fears concerning Fiona Apple. I fear I am failing you.
Sincerely,
Brian P. Case

The band he spoke of consisted of old high school friends who were not likely to ever rise to fame. Brian and his band had played in a Park City coffeehouse, the Morning Ray/Evening Star, a few years earlier, but his voice was so low, it didn't seem that there was any possibility they would excel with their music. Strangely, I can recall one incident in which I was amazed at how well he sang. Jim and I unexpectedly walked in on Brian one snowy evening when no one else was home. We stood at the door and looked at each other in amazement. Brian was singing alone with his guitar, and his voice sounded rich, full and sweet with melancholy. As soon as he saw us, he stopped. Nothing I could say would ever get him to sing again.

HOSPITALIZATION

After a few weeks with his father and Brian's constant talk of guns, hiding under the bed and obsessing over Sheryl Crow, Sam made the decision to call a mobile unit in Virginia to analyze Brian for mental illness. Sam called me first, and we agreed we needed to get a definite diagnosis. I had always suspected a "duel diagnosis" which would indicate one problem as drug addiction or "self-medication" for the other problem which was a mental cause for his erratic behavior. After six years of seeing various doctors, this was the first time we received a concrete answer that there was an identifiable problem with our son. With his own attorney, Brian had himself admitted to the psychiatric ward of Mt. Vernon Hospital so he would be able to sign himself out later on. I called him almost every day only to find him heavily drugged, depressed and apathetic. In speaking to his doctor who was foreign with a heavy accent, I learned that he was certain Brian was *schizo-affective*. He had the worst combination of being both bipolar and schizophrenic. We now knew he was ill both in his moods and in his thought patterns. He had turned twenty-one in early October of that year. Unfortunately, by age twenty-one, the law now gave him the right to refuse medication. That law basically signed and sealed his death certificate.

This is a letter from Brian's notebook, written on his 21st birthday.

Dear Emilie,

What's up? Let me guess . . . the corners of your mouth, cause you're smiling, but I can only imagine. And as for myself, well, I'm very, very lonesome out here in Virginia and today's my birthday and I'm afraid of making any friends right now, especially after how the last batch turned out. Where are the feasts I was promised?

No place. I wasn't promised shit, and I'm just wasting away in God-forsaken Virginia of all places where shit-starting is a 24/7 profession, or so it seems to me. At least I can get legally drunk from now on. That's a definite plus. Anyway, I apologize if this letter is in any way a violation of your privacy. I guess I just need an invisible shoulder to lean on right now. If only I had money or a car, not that my license is valid, but I'd take out this night with style had I any choice in the matter. I feel like Rapunzel in the Holy Grail or something.

I racked up gobs of cd's today. It's funny . . . I awake one morning in that half-way house at the very tippy-top of Main St. and opened my eyes in the precious light of August's early sun to the most strangely familiar tune, to this haunted voice and her sole guitar swaying alone beyond my fuzzy and crackling alarm clock radio. My mind left my weeping soul or maybe my soul stole my mind for awhile, then the song ended. "That was Michelle Shocked with Stillborn." I know that girl from Mr. Krenkle's class back in '96. I told him the insects in the background reminded me of eastern Texas, so he informed me of the fact that Michelle Shocked engendered there. Anyway, maybe the two of you might relate to each other. I also was given Charles Mingus' Pithecanthropus Erectus, which rocks my soul. I really dig jazz, but only certain particularities. I'm not totally gung ho like so many people I know . . . can you associate with me? Anyway, I'm consuming too much of your time, so I'd best be off now. Keep safe and God speed. All that I can and can't see happens for its own reasons. Does it for you?
Peace. Brian

After three weeks passed, Brian was allowed to leave the hospital with the drug *zyprexa*. Although Sam watched him take his daily dosage, Brian later told me he spit it out in the backyard when he went out to light a cigarette. He called me often, usually ranting and angry at his father. They would both get on the phone, yelling at each other and then at me. If I hadn't had Jim to lean on during this time, I think I would have lost touch with reality, too.

LOSS

November 27, 1998, Jim's father passed away, the day after Thanksgiving and one month before our wedding. We'd just bought a house of our own and were so happy that we could build a life together. As we flew to St. Louis for the funeral, Jim was in denial about his father's impending death. On the plane, he voiced his concerns about his father having to learn to walk and talk again after his stroke. I remember riding the escalator into the hospital, then turning around and seeing Jim frozen at the bottom of the steps, unable to take that first step. Jim was in such denial. He'd finally gotten his act together, and his father wouldn't be alive to see his achievements. He and his family were devastated by his father's unexpected death.

At midnight after the funeral, Brian called at Jim's mother's house, completely outraged and out of control. Brian was yelling at Sam to take the medicine, that he needed it more than Brian did himself. Sam began screaming in my ear, too. Since I couldn't calm either one of them down, I finally hung up the phone. They called back twice more, both screaming furiously. I kept thinking this is what he's like, even on the medication. I thought I was going to have a nervous breakdown from anxiety and fear of Brian's future.

FROM BRIAN'S NOTEBOOK IN VIRGINIA, FALL 1998:

Mom's told me she wants me to come home to stay,
Mama told Dillon she wants me to return here,
My eye hasn't stopped twitching for 4 days now,
And I've been writhing and bleeding and contorted for countless days
*   now . . .*
They are all traitors . . .
They tear me apart from the inside like poison . . .
They have poisoned my entire life . . .
They love me while they rape me . . .
They don't believe in me . . .

Dad's always boss . . .
He pulls his rank when I step out of line . . .
He doesn't like me the way I am,
Shits on me,
Told me I throw like a girl . . .
Books me in the asylum at age 21 because I've been dysfunctional too
  long . . .
So I'm psychotic due to the trauma experienced during my parents'
  divorce they say,
So now Dad tells me I'm sick and he wants me to stop throwing like a
  girl,
But I don't throw like a girl these days,
And my only friends back home are geniuses,
And enduring hell made me strong,
Strengthened my mind and personality and perception,
Something my father the fool can never conceive . . .
I'll never live with him again . . .
I'll never trust any of them ever again,
But I'll always love them and never hurt them.

Cody and Dillon flew to Virginia to spend an early Christmas there. They toured some museums and ironically, a year later, I was shaken when I put on Brian's coat and there in the pocket, I found the Van Gogh brochure from the exhibit they had seen together. I think on some level, Brian identified with Van Gogh and often painted in an imitative style. After an exasperating phone call and ensuing argument, Brian would grab his paintbrush and vent his feelings on canvas. Those paintings are powerful reminders to me of the incredible mental pain my son was suffering through as he painted.

In Virginia, Brian was supposed to be in a program in which he was driven in a van and spent part of the day participating in group counseling. He later told me the group was totally depressing with older people talking about how they'd lost their children, their homes and had their financial stability ruined. He hated the group therapy. He said it made him feel even more hopeless, and I wondered about the wisdom of the "therapy" these specialists recommended. This sounded not only ridiculous to me but smacked of idiocy, incompetence and poor judgment on the part of the doctors.

SCHIZOPHRENIA:

ONE FLEW OUT

When Brian realized Jim and I would be having a December wedding, he told the medical staff that he had to return to Utah. Sam found out there would be a wedding and immediately went ballistic. Part of his reasoning was in regard to whether or not Cody and Dillon would be able to get financial assistance for college if I remarried. I assumed that Sam would interfere somehow with the wedding, and I wanted to avoid any nasty involvement on his part, so I had kept our plans fairly quiet. Although I had made no secret of my engagement ring I'd been wearing since October, Sam typically hadn't noticed when I'd sat with him at lunch with Cody and Dillon during one of his autumn visits. Neither had he noticed the announcement in the local newspaper.

The morning he called to say he was sending Brian back to Utah, Sam phoned six times in a half-hour, while being threatening and verbally abusive. He said it was a one way ticket and that if I wanted to send Brian back to Virginia, I'd have to pay for another ticket. In the meantime, Sam went to Europe with his girlfriend and her daughters. He absolutely refused to take Brian with them. He'd even gone so far as to say he'd lock Brian in the house while he was away. I told Sam that I was sure Brian would kill himself over Christmas if he was left alone. I could not understand Sam's anger over the wedding since he had been the one to leave our marriage. I suspect it was the lack of control over my life that upset him. However, he could exert plenty of control through Brian. To his detriment, Brian was a pawn not only in his mental illness but in a disastrous divorce.

That cold afternoon in December, I was just coming in the door at four-thirty when I heard the message to pick up Brian at the airport in a few hours. I immediately tried to phone Sam back regarding the all important hospital records and his medicine but there was no answer. When I went to the Salt Lake airport baggage area, I didn't see Brian. He walked toward me and said hello, but I didn't recognize him. The medication had made him gain weight and look inflated. His face was puffy and distorted, and his hair shorter than I'd ever seen. His eyes had a strange, squinty coldness that made me wonder if aliens had taken my son and left this stranger. Even more surprising was his tendency to chain smoke. This was unbelievable coming from a kid who used to accost strangers on the street and lecture them on the dangers of smoking cigarettes.

According to *schizophrenia.com,* 90% of schizophrenics and 60 to 70% of people with bipolar disorder smoke to relieve their symptoms, raise their dopamine level and make them feel "normal" for while. A Harvard study also indicates in *schizophrenia.com* that as much as 44% of cigarettes sold in the U.S. are consumed by the mentally ill which is considered to be 4 to 8% of the population. Self-medicating with drugs and alcohol is sometimes the only thing that makes their lives bearable. Instead, by society's standards, we often see them only as spineless drug and alcohol abusers who should pull themselves up by their bootstraps and get a grip on reality. I often wonder how anyone else of my family and friends would deal with the endless sensation of hearing voices from a thousand televisions aimed constantly in their direction. Some of them indulge anyway in drugs and alcohol for recreation but, ironically, that's considered socially acceptable if you aren't mentally ill. Brian had also developed a tic in the area of one eye that annoyed him greatly. To him, it must have seemed reasonable to drink or do drugs to fog over the effects of the illness.

BACK TO UTAH

I took Brian home from the airport in mid-December and for the first time in years, he seemed calm and content. When he explored the new house and the wide-open spaces and mountain trails surrounding the area, he expressed how happy he was that we finally had our own home again. There was a stream behind the house and a rocky hillside that led up to the mountains. Right away, he wanted to go running and wander in the hills. He came back with a mellow attitude I hadn't seen in him since his childhood. That first evening, he went out with an old high school friend, and I warned them both what dangers could lie in alcohol and drugs combined with Brian's medicine. They seemed to take note and didn't stay out very late. That first night, I dreamed I floated downstairs and placed my hand on his chest while he was sleeping, that it glowed red and he was miraculously cured. I prayed to God for this miracle, to cure Brian's illness.

We had a long talk the next day. Brian sat next to me on the sofa and cried openly when he described his experiences in the hospital. He believed wholeheartedly there was nothing wrong with him, and that he was not ill but had been hospitalized as punishment by his father. He remained the sixteen-year-old rebellious teenager that was angry his father left him with two younger brothers and a mother battling depression, poverty and homelessness. He had been too young and incapable of taking on all the responsibilities of a family in crisis. Brian's psyche was frozen at that time, age 16, and rarely relented from that standpoint. He did say the doctors had talked of forgiveness and that he had to forgive all of us for being human and making mistakes. He said he was going to try to take that advice. I told him I would try to work on that goal myself despite all my resentments and anger.

One frightening moment occurred when he eagerly showed us the little paper insert from one of Sheryl Crow's cd's and explained its special message to him. He had taken all the letters and reformed them into a code that was meant only for him. When he talked of turning the "e's" sideways so they could speak to him, my blood ran cold. I remembered that as a small boy, Brian had made fun of my father who believed in UFO's and angel visits. Now I realized Brian actually believed that Sheryl Crow's music and words were written for him, an anonymous fan. My father could be forgiven his confusion in his old age, but I wondered how could my son at the prime of his life believe such ridiculous hallucinations. Brian began making phone calls and sending emails he hoped would somehow reach Sheryl Crow.

From Brian's notebook, apparently after he returned to Utah:

Dear Sheryl,
I just heard that song about how you'd descend and teach me and stuff, so I can't quite figure out why you haven't rescued me yet. Anyway, I'm guessing you're already aware that I've been relocated to my mother's house (she really wants me to get better) so now I can get on a job and pull the rock and roll band into action somehow, and then we'll relocate at the city of Angels . . .that is, if you don't rescue me first. Why did you hang up? Never mind. . .it's all my fault and I've been hating myself for quite a while now. So I apologize for being an absurd fool. At any rate, I'm back where it all began, in Park City. Please write back to me.

Brian at age 21 at home in Utah, his last Christmas, 1998.

When Brian arrived in Utah December 17th, the week before my wedding, he had a container with a half dozen pills called *zyprexa*. It became immediately clear to me that we would have a hell of a time getting the prescription filled with his father in Europe. Despite Brian's time in the hospital in Virginia, we didn't have records and would have to start over with another doctor. He would have to find a doctor in Utah, a psychiatrist who would refill the prescription. When I called for an appointment, I was told it was a two-month wait to see the doctor and that Brian had to make the appointment, as usual. I wrestled with trying to get the prescription filled through doctors Brian had already seen. They would have to see him again, of course, to prescribe meds, and they were out for the holidays. He refused to see them, at any rate, and he refused to take the medicine anyway. He insisted he didn't need any meds, and that he wasn't sick. He insisted he'd been spitting out the pills these past few months. One day when he beat the back of the chair he was sitting in, I wish I'd had a video camera. He screamed repeatedly, "I am not sick!" and swore that he would never take the medicine again. He said if he was sent back to Virginia, he would kill himself. He sounded like he meant it, too. I felt trapped along with him in his illness.

We took this photo (Dillon, Jean, Brian, Cody) on a family road trip to CA during happier times. I showed it to the counselor who insisted Brian had experienced a "shitty" childhood.

I took him to a local counseling center where they did grant an interview. Brian had them totally convinced he was fine. The counselor then spoke with me alone. He informed me that Brian was reacting to his "shitty" childhood. In his opinion, I should help him get a job and an apartment. I should "stop being overprotective and over-mothering him." I should become much less involved in Brian's life, and he would be "fine." He added, I should also keep him away from his father and be supportive of the fact that Brian didn't want to have anything to do with him. This was quite a contradiction to the doctor's reports from Virginia, but of course, we did not have those records available at the time. Brian was now twenty-one and would have to request the records himself. The information in the records was considered confidential and would not be released to parents. He did sign for them, but it took over three months before they actually arrived in Utah. By then he had relocated to Texas.

When Brian died, the same counselor phoned and told Jim he was "having a hard time with Brian's death." Jim responded tersely, "You should see the mother."

According to an earlier phone conversation I'd had with the primary care doctor in Virginia, he personally felt sorry for the father whom Brian treated so poorly. Sam came to see him everyday, yet Brian hardly spoke to him or spoke angrily when he did. By Brian's account, his father stood over him at the hospital and laughed at him. He said the attendants punished him by withholding his music and cigarettes. His father agreed this last was a true statement. Sometimes I really didn't know who to believe and who was ill, including myself, his father and the doctors.

During December and January, as long as I didn't mention the two topics of the medicine or his father, Brian proved to be comparatively easy to get along with back in the family setting. He began working bussing tables at an upscale restaurant across the street from my office at the art center. He was driving the old truck again, even though it was winter, and things seemed to smooth out for a while. It was a calm, carefree time compared to the past few years. He'd said he'd finished with drugs and alcohol, and I wanted to believe him. Although he didn't have his own room in our house, he slept on the sofa in the band/family room which adjoined to a bath and the kitchen. The boys, Jim and I had our three bedrooms and two bathrooms upstairs. Brian's appetite came back in full force, and he was often in the kitchen creating meals and snacks. We realized trying to find alternative housing for him in a ski town during the winter would be a waste of time. Christmas time meant the normal rental rates had tripled in price and were completely booked. Even so, it was good to have him home again during the holidays. We were all together as a family and preparations for the wedding made that holiday season especially exciting.

During November and Brian's hospitalization in Virginia, Jim and I had begun attending **NAMI (National Alliance for the Mentally Ill)** meetings. Although I didn't really feel this group had anything to do with us, I wanted to do some research and find out what they had to say. I learned that people like Brian were called *consumers*. We found considerable support from other parents and siblings at these meetings. The parents were going through or had gone through very many of the same phases of mental illness that we were experiencing with Brian. Still, part of me was in denial that his problem was nearly that serious. If only he would take his prescribed drugs rather than the street ones, it would be a wonderful world.

Living between denial and distraction, I had my mind on the wedding, and hoped and prayed Brian would miraculously be cured. In the back of my mind, I thought maybe the doctors in Virginia were mistaken. Maybe they had misdiagnosed him. Or maybe it was just the drugs Brian had taken that gave him such paranoia. Also, during November, I had discussed the situation with my sister in Denver along with the possibility of Brian seeking assistance there. She was aware of more and better programs in Colorado than those available, which were basically non-existent, in Utah. What did exist, half-way house type environments in Salt Lake City, had long waiting lists for people considered to be in more need of help than Brian. However, the medical staff in Virginia had quickly advised against moving Brian. They said he needed the stability of the program he was already in, and that moving him so soon could be devastating. Why that ruling did not apply in sending him back to Utah a month later made no sense to us. Apparently, it was convenient timing by then for his father's European trip.

The worse result of what I learned later from **NAMI** was that Brian should have been treated like a patient recovering from heart surgery. For six months, he should have been able to sleep day and night if he wanted to do so. Instead, he was being told to get out into the world, find a job, or several jobs, find housing and learn to survive on his own. One day when I came home and found him watching tv during his "recovery," I was angry that dishes were piled up and the house was a mess. I feel so guilty now that I demanded that he do something productive. Brian got up out of his favorite chair, began washing dishes and muttering to himself, "Get a job, get a job, get a job." He was as incapable of working at that time as anyone who'd been hospitalized for cancer, heart disease or diabetes. Our relatives called, not to ask how he was doing, but with the number one question, "Does Brian have a job, yet?"

People who meant well said comforting phrases such as: "You did the best you could. You didn't know. Schizophrenia is hard to diagnose. You can't blame yourself." To them I would say, "Oh yes, we can blame ourselves and as parents we always will. Do we ever give up on our child getting well? Do we ever think there isn't a miracle cure or one more doctor who might be the one who understands what we're experiencing—if only we could locate that one person? No, I didn't go to medical school, but I did have a mother's instincts that said my son was not just a lazy bum. He was very ill and incapable of taking care of himself. Society did nothing to help him. Social services representatives need to be educated on the reasons mentally ill people can't be responsible for getting help on their own or making and keeping appointments. The logic in the frontal lobe has shut down and other regions such as the hypothalamus try to take over the thought processes but without the advantage of logic. How can we as caretakers expect an ill person to rely on logic to protect himself, make appointments, find food and shelter or even understand why he needs to take medicine? People like Brian who desperately need help fall through the cracks in the system. That is exactly what the last counselor said, that Brian simply "fell through the cracks."

In this ski resort town where we lived, millions of dollars went to non-profit organizations that assisted the arts, sports, radio station, etc., and individuals who had physical disabilities. These programs involved expensive ski equipment, horses, rafting, etc., for the physically challenged. In contrast, my son could not get even a free meal because of the stigma of mental illness.

In our society, we can deal so much better with the illnesses we can see that exist below the neck in twisted limbs and often helpless bodies in wheelchairs. Someday, I hope we can give the same kindness, understanding and compassion to those whose minds have become twisted by disease. For the eternally skeptical, there are now tests available with sensors that indicate the workings and failures in the human brain. Even at the time, I wanted an MRI of Brian's brain to prove to myself that I didn't imagine his illness.

*Brian, left with drink in hand, agreed to sit with us for a
family wedding reception photo.*

OUR WEDDING DAY

Christmas Eve, Jim's family arrived en masse and my attention was drawn to airport pick-ups, meals and housing, along with last minute wedding details. Although her husband had died the month before, Jim's mother and his entire family were not going to let this joyous occasion be overlooked. Jim had been a bachelor since age twenty-seven, and they'd waited a long time for him to remarry. I owe them so much for making it a beautiful wedding, joining our two families and accepting my three sons and me, including all our imperfections. One of my sisters and my niece also flew in from Denver despite snowy weather and the inconvenient traveling time for the wedding on December 27th, just following Christmas.

For three evenings in a row, we fed twenty-five people for dinner with tables spread from the kitchen into the living room. Jim's best friend from childhood, Tom, and his family surprised us with their arrival from Houston. We had been through so much the past few years, it was wonderful to receive the acknowledgement and support from so many valued friends and family members.

I have photos from one of the large dinners where Brian is sitting alone on the stairs above the crowded room. He seemed to be sulking and introspective. I remember asking him if anything was wrong, and he had denied that there was. Now I think the contrast of the jovial party and his dark moods brought him down. In his mind, the comparison of the pain he'd been through in the hospital to the joy of the wedding party must have been a harsh reality of what his life had become and would continue to be in his future.

The day of the wedding, Brian reacted perfectly normally to the situation, seemingly content and happy. He'd refused my offer of hurriedly ordering him a tuxedo as his brothers were wearing. My sister had ironed a couple of nice shirts he could choose from, but instead, much to our dismay, he went out to the garage and pulled an old striped sweater from a box. The twins were walking me down the aisle, but Brian said he didn't want to participate other than to sit in church. He got through the wedding with no problem. However, at the reception, he played wild jazz music that mildly annoyed me. He also drank a little champagne and amused everyone by telling them he'd escaped from a mental hospital. Other than that distraction, he smiled into the video camera and said with complete sincerity, "Mom, I love you." What a priceless gift and memory of that day.

Jim and I postponed an official honeymoon and took only a short visit to Salt Lake City for a few days. Our lives settled into a busy routine of the boys' high school activities and jobs, plus our own work schedule. Brian had been drifting away from his restaurant work schedule until it had disappeared completely.

SUNDANCE, SLAMDANCE AND SHERYL CROW

The Sundance and Slamdance Film Festivals came to town each January, and the twins were again busy with volunteering, attending movies and parties. It was a ritual of late nights and midnight movies, and unfortunately, the inevitable array of drugs and alcohol available to anyone who could crash a party. For several years we've had a writer/ filmmaker visit us from Los Angeles. After being out with Brian one night, John confided to me that Brian was definitely back into the drug scene. I'd also heard reports that he was hanging out at a coffee shop and smoking weed with high school sophomores. His brothers were humiliated over this development.

I wrote in my diary that I especially worried about Brian's drinking and drugs during the film festival. He was very moody and obsessed with Sheryl Crow. I'd given him a poster of her for Christmas, and lacking his own bedroom wall, to our amusement, he had attached it to the back of the bathroom door. Later, when I heard how other parents said they could not change the room their deceased child had left, I was envious their child had a room. Brian didn't even have a wall to call his own. Cody and Dillon had generously shared their space with his old posters and music to the extent there was room.

Ironically, Sheryl Crow was coming to Park City to play in a local bar during the Sundance Film Festival. Brian took this as a sign that she had come for him. He was furious with the bouncers who would not let him in the bar. He waited out in freezing weather to talk to her, but she managed to leave without his being able to approach her. He was devastated with disappointment.

Recently, we found a stray letter to Sheryl written while Brian was still in Virginia. This letter is rare in that he actually mentions the possibility of schizophrenia.

. . . henceforth it is very startling and somewhat disturbing when you accurately discern my eye color, and then you go on to call out my name. But everyone thinks I'm paranoid schizophrenic, anyway, and I must agree with them that I am somewhat disturbed. So I rarely trust my judgment and I'm going out on a limb simply by writing this. At any rate, I am far from safe here in Virginia of all places so I've got to run someplace before it's too late.

Sometime during January, I found two notes he'd written that mentioned suicide in some form. He was constantly writing songs, poetry or stories. When I asked him about these obscure messages, he was not defensive, simply insisting they were just parts of songs or stories he was writing. He denied any personal interest in suicide. We had discussed the topic before, agreeing there were always other options and that suicide was too final and would hurt our family too much. Brian always seemed reasonable during these discussions, almost assuring me that I, too, would have to work out my problems.

In writing this book, I have read over many of Brian's notebooks. Lest anyone think I've overstated our relationship or that it was ever easy, I'm including a telling letter as an example of Brian's perspective. There was always just enough truth mixed in to make me feel he was not mentally ill, and it was a safer bet to blame myself for whatever was wrong with him. This letter ends with the issue of a saxophone I'd rented for Brian and had to return because I couldn't afford to keep it. This breaks my heart.

Dear Jean,

Are you never satisfied? Why hurt me? You call me a disappointment. I suppose I've failed you, but I swear to God (who most likely does not exist) that when I came alive, I intended no harm. Can you conceive tragedy? Have you ever tried thinking for yourself? Why'd you make me? Why'd you suffer to bring me into this world, understanding that I'd fear and suffer and eventually die? Possibly I'd find love and momentary pleasure. Maybe you brought me into a godless world . . . did this thought ever cross your mind? And today you told me you're suicidal. You've little reason to live these days. Fuck that shit! You are currently a coward. You have not improved at all since your divorce began so many years ago. You are very afraid, afraid to die, and you never know which day of your life is your last. You are also tragically stubborn, lost inside the caged world of the victim . . . and you are a victim, but this does not matter. Victims and heroes die alike. It is your responsibility to recover, to love one last time before your life ceases. You must try, and you must always fight. I am so pissed right now. I'm sick of our broken family, our predicament. I'm sick of the bullshit. I don't care what you think. I don't care what your victim friends say to you. You are making it worse. You are not justified, I don't care what the shrinks say. You are responsible for your actions. Wake up! When you die, it'll be too late. This is reality. We must value our time together. Don't you ever hang up the phone on me again. You refuse to acknowledge my love for music. You do not too much realize I've spent time learning this instrument. Obviously, I don't want this dream of mine to simply die. Can't you respect me at all?

*One of our last photos of Brian, taken on our
front step in late morning, January 1999.*

COUNSELING AND CHAOS

By February, things worsened considerably. Brian was returning to all his old habits of badgering the boys about taking drugs, coming home at 4 a.m. if at all, showing little to no respect for me and becoming progressively more violent in his temper tantrums. Jim and I resorted again to trying to find Brian his own apartment, although the rent in town was outrageous. We knew that we would have to pay completely for his rent, utilities, food, transportation, etc. He rarely made enough money on his own to buy cigarettes or beer. If he did have any money, he quickly gave it to homeless people he met. He did manage to get a part-time shoe store job that consisted of stocking shelves. The job was low stress and laid back enough for him to visit with other young people.

We began talking to Brian's father to get assistance. Sam was in no mood to help financially or emotionally and offered only minimal assistance. He acted like this wasn't his problem, insisting that Brian was now twenty-one, after all. I later learned from an attorney friend that I could have pursued child support for a mentally ill grown child. When I told this to his father, his answer was that I "would not get another nickel out of him." I did try to get Brian to apply for SSI and made the appointment to go with him, but he refused due to his pride. By the time the Social Security office called regarding his appointment, Brian had relocated to Texas. He mentioned many times that he didn't want to be a burden to society or to anyone else. And, once again, he could never acknowledge he had any illness. More recently, I learned that if he'd been properly diagnosed earlier, Brian could have remained on his father's government insurance for life and could have received other services as well.

Jim and I found a one-room garage apartment and showed it to Brian. It had a small kitchen area and bath adjoining one room. The rent was astronomical. To me, it was also too heavily treed, dark and depressing. I kept looking carefully at the shower arrangement that looked suitable for hanging a person. It gave me chills, and we decided against it. The location was not very accessible to town, located high in a wooded area, surrounded by family homes. Transportation problems would have been difficult for commuting to any work area or social life.

Brian was still driving his old Chevy truck or an old Isuzu painted with desert arches when either one was running which was rare in winter. Often the heaters didn't work, either. One afternoon he became angry with all of us and drove off in a fury, screaming at us in the driveway. A few minutes later, he called from the fire station where the truck had stopped running. His voice was calm, asking me to pick him up as if nothing had happened. We had learned to hide our keys and not to let him borrow our car for even a short errand into town. From experience, we knew there was the likelihood he would not only take the car but also be gone for three days and not call us or let us know where he'd gone.

As February was coming to an end, Jim and I realized this situation had worn itself out. We were both tired of the arguments among the boys and were feeling emotionally battered. We'd been married two months and agreed Brian would have to become Sam's responsibility, even though he still lived in Virginia. With Brian in our home, the other boys became more difficult to live with, too. They were out late one night when Brian had gotten so out of hand, I'd locked myself in my room. He was slamming doors and knocking pictures off the walls in his frustration. Jim came in the door and realized how afraid I was to be home alone with Brian. I was seriously considering calling the police at this point. My pride got in the way, and I didn't want to admit that I couldn't handle my own child.

The following are excerpts from Brian's notebook.

I was clever enough to uncover the lie, but I still found myself trapped
*   *. . . dead.*
And I suppose this truth is too obvious:
Only the living maintain the strength to manipulate their inertia.
Every reasonable man should seek control over his destiny
while acknowledging with head bowed, realities, certainties.
It's very important wise men recommend that you face the skull in the
*   mirror.*

The last page of his notebook reads:

Poor, poor Brian's brain fell to pieces while he was still a kid.

The universe overwhelmed him . . .
He lost it, couldn't juggle quickly enough, so reality slipped beyond his
  grip.
This was the most tragic moment of his life, consisting of innumerable
  tragedies.
Thereafter, Brian lost his imagination (a giant portion of his soul's
  constitution).
As he transformed into a zombie, his creative abilities became as unread-
  able as the sun, thus he suffocated like a man on the moon.
Somehow, he was no longer himself.
You could say he died as a child, that he never had a chance.
He found his new self disarmed of the imagination, incapable of con-
  ceiving the complexity of this irrevocable tragedy that killed him,
  left to writhe away, aimlessly in the cold, forever seeking the non-
  existent key, and he was dying all the while.
He would never live again, were it not for the blinking key, an illicit
  substance.
Once inhaled, it forced him into reality, but it stole him away just as fast.
And it sufficed for a long, long time. Until reality threw a curve ball.
He heard the soft whisper on a crescendo of wind,
speaking of humanity's last great tragedies already on the rise.
He could barely breathe.
He felt himself, limbs shaking in anticipation.
His breathing became involuntary.
Such little time left to live.

Jim and I had discussed our dilemma at length and agreed to give Brian his medicine without him being aware of it. I sought the advice of a psychiatrist who understood our impossible situation and was willing to counsel us, if not Brian. Although the psychiatrist was helpful in explaining to us the shut down in Brian's brain, he wasn't actually seeing Brian. At age 21, our son had not broken the law and was still considered "no threat to himself or society," so he could not be forced to see any more doctors. The doctor suggested we document in a diary how Brian responded to the medication in his food. Hopefully, after a month or so, we would be able to show Brian the diary and his improvement on the meds would become more convincing to him.

DIARY

February 18th, I wrote in my diary – "Things are getting worse with Brian. There are arguments in the house continually, and he refuses to take his meds. They've all worn off from his stay in Virginia. I locked myself in my room. Brian was pounding on the door, screaming and slamming pictures off the walls. I'm getting more desperate by the day. He beat up the living room chair today, screaming over and over, "I'm not sick.""

February 19th, I wrote – "Out of pure desperation I called Mary (with **NAMI**) today, and she told me to contact Craig and set up an appointment for us. I can see him next Tuesday – if I can make it until then. Between my own moods, attacks of arthritis and Brian's moods, I am beyond depressed and feeling suicidal myself. Jim and I discussed giving Brian the meds and decided to begin treating him. We bought a chocolate shake. I drank half, added the crushed *zyprexa* and casually offered it to Brian. Thank God, he took it."

February 20th, – "Brian slept late, more mellowed and easy to talk to today."

February 21st, – "Brian slept very late again. He embarrassed Dillon at the hotel where Dillon worked as a bellman. Brian stumbled out of the car with his friend, drunk and carrying beer. Then he came home and slept. He's obsessed and keeps going to the clinic and getting tested for AIDS."

February 22nd, – "We cut down the dosage from the indications on the prescription. He's working at the shoe store, seems more motivated and is actually starting conversations. He seems to be coming out of his withdrawn silence. He's not focusing on fear of contracting AIDS, herpes, etc."

February 23rd – "Brian got another job at a hamburger restaurant. He called about his car insurance and is back to driving today. In only four days, his "recovery" is remarkable. He's showing an interest in life again, more positive, not angry or picking fights, not talking in illogical circles. He seems non-aggressive and was actually singing in the shower. For the first time, I am hopeful for Brian's recovery. We saw Craig today. I feel ecstatic that Brian will be one of the few who totally recover."

February 24th – "Even better today. Brian is positive, joking, making such improvements. I am so happy thinking he will be able to have a real life—"

February 25th – "Total devastation. I was in a hurry with his medication and he confronted me angrily. How can he know he is ill and accept the meds which he believes are wrong for him, to fight his chronic illness alone? Brian will end up starving alone in the street. I am heartbroken over this. I only wanted to help him find his way. It is his choice, and he will suffer a thousand times for his illness. If I were sick with diabetes or cancer, would he let me die in the street refusing to take medication?"

I have replayed the incident over and over in which Brian caught me medicating his drink. I remember that evening I was cooking dinner. The crowded kitchen was full of the boys and their friends. The phone rang and I was distracted with a call regarding the art center and an upcoming exhibit. Instead of grinding the pill to a powder, which had to be done out of Brian's sight, I hurriedly mixed it in iced tea with sugar. I didn't realize it would sit on the bottom like a rock rather than dissolve. I was upstairs when Jim came to warn me Brian was extremely upset over the discovered medicine. He stomped upstairs and confronted me angrily. He knew immediately that I had given him the pill when he found it in the bottom of the iced tea glass. Demanding to know why I had given it to him without his knowledge, he even said he would hire a lawyer and sue me for poisoning him. He said that I had no right to give it to him without his knowledge and that I didn't understand what could happen to him because of the meds.

This was an impossible situation. In order to keep him alive and functioning, I was trying to medicate him without his knowledge. Despite all the advice of medical professionals, there was no way to get him to agree to the medicine in order to get something he wanted. Brian was stubborn beyond all reason. Now he was threatening to leave because we were in a conspiracy to "poison" him, to his point of view. He wasn't sick and didn't need medication. He thought we were all crazy. Brian hurried downstairs, packed his bag and ran out the door. He'd been threatening to leave by hitchhiking away on the interstate for the past few months. Recently, he'd met a wanderer in a cafe and was ready to go anywhere. I was terrified he would leave any safety and security with us and encounter violence or die on the road. Fortunately, this time when he was angry about the meds, he simply ran to a friend's house.

February 27th, we arranged a meeting with our long-time family counselor and Brian's father. The counselor specialized in substance abuse and domestic problems, so we hoped he could help. Although we tried to discuss all aspects of the situation, Sam soon consulted his watch and said he had a plane to catch, as usual. This had been his pat response to any problems regarding the boys for the past five years. Once again, I felt emotionally abandoned and resentful as he took off for the airport.

However, he told the counselor he would personally call to find more resources to help Brian in Utah and would see what he could do. He left with his task list but never pursued the items such as housing, counseling for Brian, etc. I left feeling angrier than I had in years. I knew with certainty that Brian's father would continue to use him as a pawn against me, controlling my life and whatever happiness I might have in my second marriage through the way he treated our son. If Jim hadn't sat between my ex-husband and me, I felt I could have reached over and shaken some sense into this self-absorbed man who had fathered my children. Nothing had changed. He had developed a pattern of being emotionally disconnected and physically distanced from the family's problems that mimicked the way he had lived with all of us together in earlier years.

PREMONITION

Sometime during this winter, I vividly remember Brian and I were talking in the living room. It was a warm afternoon, flooded with sunlight bouncing off new fallen snow outside the windows. When we turned any corner in our house, we never knew what mood Brian would be in or what to expect. That afternoon, we made a mental connection on some level. He asked me very calmly when the year 2000 would arrive. This would have been something he understood when he was younger and more aware of time. I patiently explained that January 1st, 2000 was considered to be the change to the new millennium. He shook his head and said he'd never make it until then. When I asked what he meant, he extended his hand and showed me his very short lifeline. I tried to cover my understanding of what he meant and denied that a short line on his palm meant anything. He spoke very softly and looked directly into my eyes. We reached some understanding of his death, but I looked away. I couldn't bear to think he would really die. I remained in total denial despite any and all direct warnings.

There had been times during the previous summer when Brian was barefooted and had refused to get in the car, thinking I might take him to a hospital. His trust level was zero. Other times he'd tried to jump out of the car moving at seventy miles per hour or grab the steering wheel while I was driving. For at least a year after the last frightening accident, I had not been in a car with Brian driving. He had threatened to kill both of us while driving crazily up the canyon, speeding and passing recklessly. Then suddenly he'd calmed down and acted like everything was fine. I'd been shaking when I'd gotten out and swore I'd never ride with him again.

I realized when I found this poem in Brian's notebook that he wrote it the last time I'd ridden with him driving.

Ode to Mommy

Stirred souls listened,
And cried,
With sympathy and compassion,
For their soul flights.
She swerved across the dotted line,
With clouded eyes,
Alive in the mysterious night of the blistering
Beating of Irish tongues.
Bags and pipes awoke her.
And steered her across the line,
Or she steered herself.
Who's to say?
But now I'm behind the wheel,
With dry eyes,

While she cries,
Inside the musical coffin
Of a blue Mitsubishi Eclipse
I carry her along
Swerving the lane
Night roads and through the mountains' breasts
And I drive too fast.

One February afternoon I drove up to the house and found Brian outside in the yard. I lured him into the car with promises of going out to dinner. He was in one of his better moods and less suspicious than usual. This particular afternoon I was able to drive him to Salt Lake City without incident. I'd been on the phone all morning to arrange a meeting with a psychiatrist at the University of Utah. The doctor that had been recommended was not available so I was shifted to someone else. We reached the University of Utah Neuropsychiatric Institute and found the correct office. It was late in the day, and the doctor I had originally requested was actually at the front desk playing solitaire on the computer. He reassured me that he had too many clients and the doctor we were scheduled to see would work out well for us. He did say the doctor's personality was a little crotchety but that if we stuck with him, he would help us. I was struggling to feel optimism over sheer panic.

When we met the assigned doctor, he curtly directed us to chairs, proceeded to fire questions at Brian, never looked up and totally concentrated on putting Brian's answers into his data base. Brian tended to mumble, another sign of his mental disorganization, as he spoke which didn't help the older man's hearing. The few times I bothered to interject or clarify what Brian said, the doctor glared at me over his glasses and asked me to not interrupt. One question was for Brian to explain the saying, "While the cat's away, the mice will play." Brian took off on some philosophical jaunt of when the Nazis were not looking, the Jewish people would break all the rules. This was about the only time the doctor actually looked directly at Brian and asked him to explain his comment. The doctor seemed exasperated and tried to get him to change his answer. He asked Brian why he was there, and he responded that he was doing this for his mother and for dinner. When he asked Brian what he liked to do, he answered that he liked to eat.

The doctor suggested Brian might take his medication, but he replied with a definite no thanks. He said he did not like the side effects and did not need the medicine since he wasn't sick. The old doctor then said if he ever changed his mind, to let him know. As we were leaving the room, out of Brian's hearing, I quietly asked the psychiatrist if he thought Brian was schizophrenic. He said he thought Brian was depressed, but he "hoped he wouldn't read his obituary in the newspaper." The reality of that premonition shook me since we had been there for less than an hour. As we exited to the hall, under his breath Brian said bluntly in reference to the doctor, "Asshole." We went to have Brian's favorite seafood dinner and again, I wondered who was least in touch with the real world. Later when I got a bill for $110 from this particular doctor, I sent him the obituary.

By March, I had developed the attitude of it's me or him, regarding Brian. We were all worn down emotionally. The violent arguments became a daily occurrence. Brian had attacked me for something as ridiculous as my Texas accent. He would react with hatred and scorn over some insignificant flaw. With his brothers, there was a continuing battle over sound systems, cd's, the phone and cars. The younger boys had earned money and with their father's help, they'd bought a nice car which infuriated Brian. I often looked from the window upstairs at the shiny red Subaru parked next to the rusty old pick-up and the beat up Trooper we called the "Archmobile." The twins and their friends drove to California for spring break and refused to take Brian, no matter how much I begged them to give us a break. They needed to get away. I'm ashamed to say I actually fantasized they would leave him there and he would miraculously get the help he needed. I envisioned progressive psych programs in California that would likely take decades to reach Utah.

March 4, 1999 – This was the last day I saw Brian. We took him to the airport, agreeing he could fly to Albuquerque then on to Austin. I bought the ticket and gave him all the cash I had to spare. At this time, my left foot was twisted with arthritic pain, and I could not walk with him all the way to the gate. I gave him a tight hug, tried to smile, told him to get his act together and come home again. I sat down and sobbed as Jim walked him to the plane.

When we left the airport, I could tell Jim was elated. We'd had our share of arguments over Brian's future, and Jim could only feel relief. It felt like a rock had settled in the pit of my stomach. I instinctively knew I would never see Brian again. I kept thinking we should hurry back and get him off the plane. The accusations that loomed in my mind were that I had been guilty of being overly protective and of over-mothering my son.

"The Will"

I know I'm right to lead my life,
Although I've lost my mind,
And though I fear the worst is here,
My driver's license expired in due time,
As a reminder . . . So it goes, descends and darkens,
As I'm revolving about a mechanized light,
Were I lucky enough to observe?
As the clocktower strikes midnight just before Jesus arrives,
Yet again, and our past is dead and forgiven,
I'd shiver to the bone at the sight of the light in the still and the cold,
Regardless, in the memory of friendly company,
Still not alone,
And everything would still be alright.

The above poem was found several months after Brian's death. It was a crumpled note lost behind the dresser in Cody's room. I know it was months that had passed before I had the energy to attempt a thorough cleaning. The heading indicated it was meant for Brian's good friend and former roommate.

DECEMBER 22, 2000

I've escaped work for a few days for the holiday season. Sometimes working at the park seems interminably slow with time on my hands, and my mind inevitably becomes obsessed with thoughts of Brian. The overwhelming loss of Brian is too much tonight. I had been planning to make Christmas cookies, but now the thought seems abhorrent. The tree is decorated, candles are lit, the roof is sparkling with icicle lights. Still, it all seems so wrong because he isn't here to share the season with us. I'm obsessed with examining photos, always looking for some obscure clue. Piles of photos surround me on the sofa and floor.

Cody is home from college so that gives me purpose in making Christmas "normal." I can hear him strumming his guitar in his room upstairs. He's playing at a coffeehouse later tonight. I flip through cookbooks, surveying recipes, wondering at the favorite ones that have disappeared. A long white envelope falls out of an old cookbook and slides to the floor. I pick it up and see it is blank and sealed. I start to throw it away, then check inside. A yellowed page unfolds in my hands. A child's drawing of a tree and Santa are proudly displayed. The imperfect spellings of *Santa Cloths, chimny and Christmos* make me smile. I shake my head in disbelief, holding this fragile, artistic creation from Brian's childhood. Cody comes downstairs and looks in amazement at the drawing. Why wasn't it the Easter bunny?

Holidays seem to be the worst for grieving the loss of a loved one. There is always their favorite day or cake or decoration or music that poignantly reminds you they are no longer here to share the holiday. As if the reminders aren't enough, I find myself tortured with the modern advantage of videos. Often, late at night, I will find an excuse to watch the many videos I recorded of the boys' childhood years. It seems so natural for Brian to walk into the room at different ages, as a toddler or youngster or teenager. Sometimes, I really believe he's never left me, that he lives on if only I insert the video and turn on the tv. Some of these are highly entertaining versions of school assignments, imitation newscaster shows, puppet shows, birthday parties, and on and on with recordings of his life. This first Christmas after Brian's death, I found tiny, delicate eight millimeter tapes and played them on a dusty old projector. There I was at twenty-seven, with long, dark hair, holding Brian as a bald-headed baby and showing off my somewhat slender stomach and his chubby one. I look amazingly young, happy and animated, smiling and laughing as my sister ran the camera. Watching this, I cried until I was empty of tears.

CHRISTMAS 2000

It's 4 a.m. and I'm finding it impossible to sleep. Brian is so much on my mind tonight. I run through the "what-if" list as if he'd just died. His loss eats at me like an unending disease of craving his existence.

The pain ravages my soul on a daily if not hourly basis. My mind cannot accept the reasons nor the negligence that caused his death. I am wracked with a fury I don't know how to expend.

How do we heal from the loss of a child? Just wait for the interminable passage of time that is utterly cruel and so very slow. Will time ever block out the thousands of memories that haunt me day and night? If I could only go back two years, then what? If I had killed myself in protest, would someone finally have noticed Brian needed help? How do you persuade people to care about a mentally ill child of twenty-one? His father, various doctors and experts who tell the mother she needs to be medicated for being over-protective . . . I wonder, are those people staying awake tonight?

JANUARY 3, 2001

I've just visited the cemetery for the first time this year. The road there is icy, a blanket of snow covers the graves and headstones on the hillside. I scoop out the snow so that I can see Brian's name. On the headstone, there is a carving of mountains and a deer waiting beside a stream. Sometimes I think he is waiting patiently for me to join him. The bright red of garish, plastic poinsettias clash against the whiteness. A snowball bush we planted last spring sticks out of the snow, barren and scrawny. It reminds of the summer days when I would hear the tinkling of bells carried on the warm breeze. There on the green hillside, I would release a balloon into the air and hear the mysterious bells for no identifiable reason.

The sky is brilliantly blue today in contrast to all the snow. Cars drive swiftly past the cemetery, people with cell phones on their way to somewhere. There are skiers visible on distant slopes. I leave the car radio playing *Enya* so that Brian can appreciate the music we once shared. I wonder if I've disturbed all the old sleeping miners, pioneers and cavalry who are laid to rest there. Surely they will forgive my music for my son. My feet are numb with cold and wet as I trudge back to the car, carrying a dead autumn bouquet from Thanksgiving.

After one and a half years, I'd think logically the pain would lighten but it remains like a solid rock in my chest. My breath is shallow as if a deep flexing of my ribs would cause excruciating pain. I go through my daily routine comatose, unfeeling and unconcerned of the events around me. There is a layer of superficiality to just get through the day–pretend to breathe, pretend to laugh and rarely cry any more while going through the motions of life, yet each moment is crystallized in importance.

Some days I stop driving on my way to work at the park to see the diamond-like display of sunlight on new fallen snow. At the mall, my senses focus on the face of a newborn passing in a stroller. Sometimes I imagine that incredibly, the baby will be Brian. When I return home, my puppy's happy, slobbering greeting and warm body struggling against me with soft, sleek fur absorbs my attention. Seeing the faces of my twin sons at the momentary flickers of happiness or pain that shows in their eyes leaves marks on my soul. They steal my heart.

JANUARY 26, 2001

My 50th birthday arrives and there is an overwhelming emptiness that none of the boys are home. Dillon is studying in Prague and Cody in Santa Barbara. My friends give me a party, present me with snowshoes and read letters from the boys. I'm distracted by the thought that Brian should have sent word to me, also. I recently found the last card he gave me on my 48th birthday. It was predominantly pink, sweet and flowery. He'd written in his unmistakable scrawl, "No one deserves happiness more than you, Mom." The irony overwhelms me.

It reminded me of an argument we had the last few months of his life. I was angry that he was no longer working, just sleeping all day, eating, then going out all night. He was non-compliant in taking any prescriptive medication but willing to take any drugs off the street. When I came home from work, frustrated at his lifestyle, we had a confrontation. He quickly became explosive asking me, 'What were you thinking, bringing me into this world?" I tried to convince him he was such a wanted baby. His father and I had waited seven years into our marriage before

Brian was born. No child was ever more wanted and anticipated. He laughed at me, scorning his father. He demanded to know if someone else was his biological father. He said he'd always thought no one could treat him the way his father did, not his real father. Once in a while, he would refer to Darth Vader and mimic the tone of "son" that Vader used in speaking to Luke Skywalker. *Star Wars* having been the movie we'd watched the night Brian was born struck me as sadly ironic.

Brian was caught in the world he'd lived in mentally at age sixteen. He saw himself as physically and mentally well, competent, capable of working and attending college. He was literally frozen at a time when he had control over his world. The summer he was fourteen, he had attended the University of Utah for an environmental science class. At sixteen, he was a brilliant student and gifted track star, although his parents were getting divorced. Overnight, the foundations of his world cracked, shook and fell apart.

I remember an argument Brian had with his father in the living room of the home where we then lived. The subject of the argument escapes me other than a show of rebellion on Brian's part. His father was determined to show him who was boss, taking him by the shoulders and setting him down hard on the floor. When his father said he was grounded, Brian went directly to his room. I checked on him shortly after, finding the window wide open and snow swirling into the room. I went back upstairs and asked Sam where he thought Brian was. He immediately said Brian was in his room because he was grounded. He looked amazed when he went downstairs and found him gone. To his credit, Sam did go out and drive in a blizzard, looking for Brian. After running for hours, Brian finally wandered back home. He barely mentioned the incident and ignored the grounding.

FEBRUARY 16, 2001

Today the world learned that cloning is not only a possibility, it is an inevitability. This is an incredible thought to me. If I used one of Brian's hairs from those I saved in his baby book, will he come back to us without schizophrenia? What if I had another baby that looked just like Brian? How would I feel as a mother to have a baby identical to the young man we had lost? I am intrigued and terrified with the possibilities.

MARCH 12, 2001

Jim and I flew to Prague to visit Dillon who is studying in the Czech Republic. He greets us at the airport, and I'm struck that he's growing into a man so quickly since he left in November. I worry that he's obsessed with European culture and won't be able to assimilate into the U.S. after a year abroad. He's developed a fondness for beer, wine and fried cheese. Although he's studied the language, he's more interested in the women and the nightlife, in my observation. I wonder if he will be happy in any U.S. university next year, compared to the education of life.

APRIL 6, 2001

Today my father died due to complications from diabetes and pneumonia. At 86 years, he was in a great deal of pain so it was appropriate that his time had come. He'd survived poverty and picking cotton as a child, Pearl Harbor, one wife and four kids during a long, full life. One of the last things he asked as he became weaker was to identify the man standing in the corner. My sister replied that the air conditioner repairman had been in the room and left. Dad said no because the man had said he loved him so much. This exchange was a comfort to me. Somehow I knew it was Brian coming to get his grandfather as death neared. Brian always expressed how much he loved us. The fact that my father was dying and going to see Brian again gave me a great sense of peace over his death.

JUNE 15, 2001

We drove to Santa Barbara to pick up Cody from UCSB. It was so wonderful to get out of Utah and a recent snow in June. At nineteen, almost twenty, Cody is becoming a man in thought, word and appearance. He is a globally conscious social activist and reminds me how I've let so much awareness and many beliefs slip away that I thought were worth fighting for thirty years ago. Attending his friends' Alternative Graduation was a moving experience that left me thinking of Brian's goals and aspirations that evaporated with his illness. He had graduated from high school through the alternative ed program, along with other students who had difficulty completing their work. His ambitions in the field of environmental science had fallen away years before graduation.

In Santa Barbara, these were high-achieving environmental science graduates, exceedingly aware of the impact our country has on the world. Cody has reminded me that the United States consumes most of the world's resources with only a small amount of the world's population. Things really haven't changed much since the early 1970's. I was touched that one parent gave his graduating child a hardbound copy of Rachel Carson's *Silent Spring*. Cody was surprised that I, too, have saved a copy of that book. Hearing the pride in the voices of these parents whose sons and daughters were arrested for protesting their various political causes reminded me of my own youthful idealism that had faded with time.

Ironically, that time had been in Austin, Texas, during 1971-1972. Having escaped my little East Texas town and a potential long term existence of being a telephone operator at the local phone company, I was deliriously happy with my freedom – mentally, physically and emotionally. I would not be marrying the boy down the street and spending my life in a closed-minded, redneck little town. Austin was the epitome of "free-thinking" in Texas. I actually participated in a protest march against the Viet Nam War, even in Texas. It was liberating to be able to think for myself and act on those thoughts. My girlhood had been measured by the southern standard of being "sweet," staying in the corner and keeping quiet. I was ill-matched for this level of sweetness from the beginning. When the other little girls wore frilly dresses in first grade or brought their prissy dolls to school, I insisted on wearing jeans because I could play more easily on the playground with the boys. Instead of being compliant as I grew older, I was caught in a world of independent thoughts that had nowhere to go.

I met my future husband in Austin. He admired my independence that had brought me to the University of Texas. Within a year, we married, and he proceeded to methodically eradicate that independent spirit as well as remold me over the next few decades. Austin had symbolized love, happiness and freedom. The beautiful setting was such a fond memory of my youth. It holds such irony that Austin was the location of my son's death. Life does indeed go full circle.

JULY 10, 2001

Dillon returned from Europe this evening. We met him at the airport with a reunion of friends and family. Foolishly imitating the celebrations of the Mormons for their returning missionaries, we brought signs and balloons to mark this occasion, greeting him at the gate at the airport. Dillon's hair is long and scraggly, his body is muscled and filled out. His head is full of new and different worldly ideas. He and his brother argue and discuss various aspects of communism, literature, languages, wine, women and world politics. If only Brian could be here, too.

LOOKING BACK

Brian had left us for Texas in the spring of 1999, and continually struggled with any sense of stability. However, the recent discovery of a misplaced note is comforting in that he was optimistic about relocating to Austin.

Sorry Mom—
Something's wild in my soul
It ain't gonna die
Call it freedom
Call it <u>Texas</u>
–Gotta know if the grass is greener
–Let me sleep in
–Let me awaken
–Let me arise to the occasion
Let me <u>LIVE</u>

Reality set in after only a few weeks. Brian realized he couldn't find a job or stay with friends in Austin, then moved to Houston for the month of April. I will be forever grateful to my sister for supporting him that month and making his life as rewarding as possible. She found him an efficiency apartment and stocked it with food. Every day she entertained him with motorcycle and boat rides as well as fine dining experiences. She laughed with embarrassment at one appetizer buffet that apparently Brian thought was the main course as he piled his plate with shrimp. My sister was able to give him all the things we couldn't afford. Unfortunately, it didn't make any difference to his recovery or survival. Maybe this soft transition bought him some time but didn't bring about any real change.

Despite my sister's kindness, Brian wasn't showing any signs of improvement. He made a few failed attempts to refinish the deck of her house and to look for a job. She wrote to me that without his friends, she didn't think he would ever be happy in Houston. Although she had originally said she would pull every string to get the medical help he needed, he refused to see any more doctors. He asked her for money for cigarettes and beer that she refused to finance. After a month, she lost patience with his lack of initiative. She was of the thinking that you teach a man to fish, not that you keep feeding him indefinitely.

Brian called me in an angry mood, saying that he was again being evicted from his apartment. I reminded him that his aunt had agreed to one month of helping him, no more. Still, he was not ready to give up his new home and move out again. I recently found a note in his scrawl that said he "would have my things out by nightfall," signed Brian Case. That note had been written at the apartment near the University of Utah a few years earlier. Being uprooted was an endless pattern for him. No one could support or live with him and his illness for very long.

Another letter he wrote near the end says it all from Brian's insightful perspective:

When every single loved one of yours turns against you, you tend to lose any sense of will-power or drive to carry on. You cease to care for yourself, and your life turns into nothing more than a project . . . testing the boundaries of your loved ones' love. I realize that my family loves me, and yet their only true desire is to cleanse their hands of me. I have transformed into a monster in their eyes. I am sick. If I am not schizophrenic, I am a con artist. Or maybe, just maybe, I'm sick from the starvation throughout some number of months last winter. Maybe I'm sick of the reality of this betrayal, that no one was there for me when I needed them most. That when I (for my own secretive reasons) was down, too down, and couldn't lift myself up, the only feasible solution my FAMILY could possibly derive was to institutionalize me and label me crazy. Suppose I was driven mad by love deprivation. No bother . . . we'll just title him sick and crazy, and henceforth usurp any will he may have possessed to carry on, and we'll usurp his sense of direction and cloud his mind with fucking drugs and we'll tell him exactly where to go – back to Virginia, back to the institution, because he has obviously, predictably relapsed.

You will never share your soul with my own, and you will never value our time together. Rather, you'll wish me away and plot and scheme until you finally succeed. My soul is writhing ceaselessly from the torment bestowed upon it, and the rain never lets up. I guess you're right – I had my chance, I had many chances and I blew them all, but if you cared to work this out like a couple of adults and stop belittling my intelligence and conspiring behind my back, I'd appreciate it.

Today, I think what a failure it was on our part, as parents, teachers, doctors, attorneys and social services, that Brian was continually dislocated, without income or any basic care and finally, to the point that he felt all alone in the world. The studies of violent schizophrenics indicate the occurrences of violence are much higher for young white males, unemployed and homeless. Brian fell through the cracks in the system. Because he wasn't violent to anyone except himself, he received little notice from the police. He never made media headlines through a violent shooting. There was no help for him that he or I could find from any government agency. Brian died by neglect. He simply slipped away from us.

This makes one realize there are thousands of mentally ill patients who die in the streets who do not make the headlines. We've witnessed too many shootings, fed by a media frenzy, focusing on acts of violence. The deaths of the non-violent mentally ill may be labeled accidents, or overdoses or even shootings by the police. President Reagan signed the law that left thousands of mentally ill people homeless, released from required medication and on their own to survive in the streets. Reagan developed Alzheimer's disease. As a society, would we turn out thousands of elderly ill patients into the streets, knowing they could not fend for themselves? The only difference is we realize these people are too old to survive and yet, we expect the young will somehow pull themselves together, apply themselves with a roll of paper towels and a bottle of spray, cleaning windshields to bring them out of their poverty. The Humane Society is kinder to animals.

LATE APRIL, 1999

Brian had left Houston by bus and returned to Austin. He had hopes of living with old friends from Utah who had relocated to Austin. This arrangement worked out for only a few days when they asked him to leave. I learned later that middle-aged co-workers actually owned the house where the friends rented. One friend had gotten a very financially rewarding computer job, and the other filled the position as the passive guest who was most likely to clean house.

Brian called us and said he'd been thrown out of his friends' house. At midnight, he was calling from outside a store that was turning off the lights. He was laughing hysterically, saying he would have to sleep in the park. I was scared for him. There was the danger of his getting beaten up or murdered in the park. I told him to return to the house and sleep in the yard or car if necessary. He wasn't listening to anything I said, and I felt overwhelmed with fear for his safety. I considered calling the Austin police but knew they would do nothing to pick up a homeless young man over twenty-one just because his mother was worried. There was also the catch that he would never tell me where he was.

Early the next morning I argued with Jim about Brian's hopeless situation. I insisted that I would drive to Austin and find him. I hadn't slept all night with worrying over what would happen to Brian. His future was looking more and more hopeless and desperate. I was overwrought with anxiety and hysterical with worry. Jim got me to calm down and said we should talk to Sam about going to Austin to find Brian. Jim definitely didn't want me to take off from Utah in a snowstorm when I was so tired and panicked with anxiety. Jim tried to call Sam in Virginia but was told he was away on a business trip. He left a message for Sam to return the call as soon as possible.

After Brian died, the woman who owned the home where he'd stayed so briefly called the day of the funeral to say she was sorry – that she had lived with a depressed father for many years and couldn't be around Brian's moods. She had offered him a plane ticket if he would leave, but he'd refused. I asked her why she hadn't simply picked up the phone and called me. She had no answer.

SATURDAY, MAY 1, 1999

Brian had called from Austin just as we were getting ready to go out that evening, and I was so happy to hear from him. He seemed to be in fairly good spirits although his voice sounded so flat. Now he planned to go to a youth hostel that I had suggested, thinking he would find help there. He talked about working at the University of Texas, getting in-state tuition and finding housing there. I felt lighthearted as we drove to the museum for a job-related art ball, thinking finally he would get help and settle into a solution for his homelessness. In my mind, I was dealing with a normal person who could get his act together if he tried hard enough. I was responding with denial in self-defense to a situation over which I had no control. Our photo was taken that evening, in which we were dressed up and looked obliviously happy in our three-month marriage. That is the last photo of that era of our lives when there was still naïve hope and optimism that things that were wrong could be righted.

MONDAY, MAY 3, 1999

This was the last time I spoke to Brian. He seemed very down and angry. His father had wired him $40 when Brian was expecting much more, which was usually a few hundred. He already owed two nights at a youth hostel, costing $17 per night, leaving him with $6. My ability to forward him instant cash was a problem. We were struggling financially and there wasn't any extra money available. The timing and circumstances couldn't have been much worse than they were that particular day.

I had come home from work at the art center in a hard snowstorm that afternoon. I'd turned on the stove and the small blue flames immediately died out. There was a notice on the door that the gas was being shut off for non-payment until I paid $370. This was Monday evening. In the stack from Friday's mail, I found a bill which had been mailed to my previous post office box, then re-routed. This was a bill from when we had lived in the low-income apartment and could be paid in small increments but that payment had to be on time. Without a phone call or other notice, we now had no heat or stove for cooking. I was so angry, I took a photo of the outdoor thermometer and the snow falling in the background. I wish I had never told any of this to Brian. I feel so ashamed that I burdened him with my anger and anxiety over the shut off heat. It was a replay of the many times our utilities and phone had been disconnected during the past few years, and the same old anxiety attack had kicked right back into gear. He even expressed his hopeless belief that "It just never ends." I asked if he would be able to call me back for Mother's Day, and he asked when that was. He replied he would call me Sunday. Then he said he loved me and hung up. He told each of us he loved us one last time.

MAY 5, 1999

Incredibly, I was quoted in a Mother's Day article regarding single moms in our local newspaper, *The Park Record*. These were my exact words in the article, "It's a character builder, you're a lot stronger than you ever thought you were. It's important to believe in yourself—take help when it's offered. You feel so proud that you don't want people to help you."

MAY 6, THURSDAY

For lunch, I finally met Vicki Cottrell, the director of **NAMI** in Salt Lake City. Although I had attempted to phone the NAMI office for months, I had not been able to connect other than by leaving messages. Vicki was attending a conference in Park City, and my friend Mary arranged for us to get together. After months of trying to reach Vicki's office while they were in the transition of moving, I was able to pin her down and get some answers about schizophrenia. She invited me to attend her class in "A Journey of Hope" at the University of Utah that evening. I rode down to Salt Lake City with her and met other parents and relatives of mentally ill persons who were coping with the same problems I faced with Brian. That night, I learned there was a good chance that some of the symptoms of Brian's disease would begin to disappear when he reached about fifty years of age. That new information fascinated me. Great, I thought. If we can keep him alive for thirty years, then maybe he can go back to college at fifty. I was actually elated at this news which I hurried home to report to Jim. Ironically, Brian had died the day before, but I wouldn't know for several days.

MAY 7, 1999

That Friday, I called Brian's father in Virginia and insisted that he had to go to Austin to find Brian. I was becoming more and more worried that we hadn't been hearing from him. My ex-husband and I got into a particularly frustrating argument on the phone. I slammed down the receiver at my office. I felt helpless and totally frustrated with Sam's indifference. It turned out that Brian was already dead when we had that last argument. I've often wondered if he could hear us.

MAY 9, MOTHERS' DAY 1999

For many years, I dreaded the celebration of Mothers' Day. It seemed to be something concocted by Hallmark, restaurants, cheap jewelry stores and, somehow, always made me feel less than worthy. Through advertising, our society had developed this bionic super mom fantasy heroine who could do it all, have it all and make it all better for everyone. She could bring home the bacon, fry it up in the pan and look great while doing so. I couldn't compete with this successful career woman image while being a stay at home mom and raising my own children. I absolutely hated having that mirror held up in front of me. Still, I cherish a gaudy gold heart necklace with a huge purple stone that Brian chose and gave to me on Mothers' Day when he was a little boy.

By 6 p.m. on this particular Mothers' Day, Brian had not called, and I was getting nervous. When the phone rang, I grabbed for it, only to hear the boys on another phone answering their father's voice. I was irritated that this was supposed to be "my day," yet he had to get into a long discussion on my time. After a half-hour, I asked them to hang up. Another fifteen minutes passed, and I was getting furious. Finally, I demanded that Cody hang up the phone, that I was still waiting to hear from Brian. Then, he and I got into a strong verbal fight. He said I was trying to keep him from seeing his father. I was laughing at this accusation. Since I hadn't been the parent who moved across the country, I failed to see how his absence was my fault. This developed into the worst fight I'd ever had with my son. So, here it was "Mother's Day," and I was crying, wishing the day would end. Inside my guts, I knew something was wrong with Brian when he didn't call. In the end, we learned it was exactly the time of day when Brian's body was discovered in Austin.

MONDAY, MAY 10TH, 1999 - THE NEWS

Still no word from Brian. The phone rang late that night, at 11 p.m. as we were going to bed. A man's voice told me he was with the Salt Lake City police. I looked directly into the hall and could see Cody and

Dillon in my line of vision. I wasn't overly concerned that they were in any trouble since they were home. The voice asked me several times if I was Brian's mother, and I confirmed that I was. Then he told me calmly, as if he were reading a weather report, the Austin City police had reported that Brian had died of drowning. I began screaming and beating the phone against the pillows. "No, no," I screamed, "You don't understand. He has schizophrenia." The last I heard from the policeman's voice was "Oh, are you alone?" Jim took the phone away from me and continued asking questions. He held onto me like he'd never let go but I felt myself sliding to the floor.

Dillon stood at the door of my bedroom, white-faced with shock. He ran into Cody's room to tell him Brian was dead. Then they both stood there, helpless and scared. We all went downstairs sobbing, with Jim practically carrying me. The boys sat in silence while I made the phone call to their father. He had called earlier from a hotel in South Dakota and, fortunately, the phone number was on the caller identification. He seemed to be awakened by the phone, so I tried to tell him as gently as possible. I will never forget the sound of his voice screaming, "No, no, no."

Jim and I called the Austin City police to find out whatever they could tell me. Brian's body had been found about 6 p.m. the evening of Mother's Day in Town Lake, now renamed Ladybird Lake. He'd obviously been in the water for several days. There was a suicide note in his pocket and no sign of foul play that caused his death. There was an indication he'd used drugs earlier but that had not been the cause of his death. The detective said nothing had happened to him before he entered the water that would give any reason for his death other than suicide. When the autopsy report arrived some weeks later, I poured over every detail. As horrifying as the details were, there was no indication he had met with violence at the hands of someone else or any possibility of overdose. I have thanked God a thousand times for the couple that found the body and contacted the police. Otherwise, I would assume he'd disappeared or been killed, and we'd never have known the truth of what happened to him. My heart goes out to parents who wait and wait, not knowing what has happened to their children who've disappeared.

As it had been Mothers' Day, there were many people in the area of the lake and the park. A man was fishing on a kayak with his dogs when he discovered Brian's body. Since he couldn't believe what he was seeing, he went to get his wife. She immediately called the police. Although there were people all around, no one else had noticed. Joggers passed by on the path. A couple sat kissing on a bench. The police roped off the area and pulled Brian's body to shore.

In the police report, there were pages of statements by the young people staying at the hostel. Most of the statements were to the effect that they were afraid of Brian, that he'd been living in a car, and that he argued loudly on the phone with his father. For two days prior to his being missing, he had continually talked about killing himself. No one paid him any attention. The news of the shootings at Columbine High School in Colorado were still constantly being aired on tv and that is what Brian would have been watching the days prior to his suicide. Unbelievably, the counselor at the hostel who might normally have helped Brian was on vacation.

The night we received the news, we spent hours talking through our shock, then I lit candles and prayed. I had been praying for protection for Brian all his life, but now I asked God for peace and comfort in his passing. The boys finally wandered back to bed for a few hours, emotionally exhausted. Jim held onto me, and we stayed awake all night. I called my two sisters but waited until the morning to tell my parents. After that, Jim took on the gruesome task of phoning friends and relatives. I will never forget this giant of a man, strong and tough beyond belief, standing in the kitchen, making phone calls with his voice breaking and tears in his eyes. Both of my sisters flew to Utah the next day and helped arrange the funeral. My brother has never said a word, sent a card or letter or expressed any comment or condolences regarding Brian's death. He had told Brian to never call him again, and Brian didn't. I realize my brother suffers with some aspect of guilt complex but that is no comfort to me even after years have passed.

I hold no one personally responsible for Brian's death. If there would be anyone to blame, it would be the parents, myself and my ex-husband, and our estranged, frustrated communication with each other. How different things might have played out without all the personal conflicts involved. Brian still may have died, but possibly, the progression of his illness could have been less painful for him and for all of us. If there is one thing I could have changed, it would have been unified support for comforting his tortured soul rather than such division among family members and friends.

Those first days, my nerves felt exposed on top of my skin. I hurt from the core of my being to the surface of my skin. Jim took me on his newspaper route early that first morning, afraid to leave me alone. As the sun came up in the mountains, a magnificent sunrise poured its golden pink beauty across the horizon. I remember doubling over with the sharpest pain in my stomach, almost like childbirth, as the slightest reality of losing my son by suicide cut through the fog of denial in my brain. I told Jim it was like the reversal of bringing life into the world; it was the grief of taking it away. Nothing in being a parent had ever prepared me for this cutting, sharp grief or this kind of unbearable loss. Only a small part, an inkling of relief for the pain Brian had been going through came over me. How terribly alone, penniless, dislocated and hopelessly depressed he must have been that his illness drove him to take his own life.

We learned later of his attempts to call each one of us May 5th before he died. He'd tried to reach his father the night of May 4th and left a message, but his father did not return the call as it was very late when he returned to the hotel in South Dakota. Brian had tried to call collect to my sister's office in Houston late in the afternoon of May 5th. The new receptionist refused to accept the collect phone call. There were three out-of-area attempts on my home phone caller identification that day. The phone card in his wallet had one credit left on it when I checked it days later.

The following poem may have been Brian's last – the final entry in his notebook.

"Shun"

My hand withered till fragile and slight,
Lost to the break of day,
I was already sunk, but still sinking when I glimpsed the light,
That I'd never find my way away from this maze,
Out of this haze,
That I wasn't bred tough enough,
That I was lame and I'd lost anyway,

To the game I couldn't even play.
That is the way it goes . . .
The way of this world.
This sad, sad mold.
Of the clay my world sold.
Who's even to frame?
Be it for guilt or for blame?
For all I could have been,
I've done nothing to my own end,
But betray my family and friends,
And accumulate shame.
I am nothing now,
Inflated and cracked in the heat of the kiln,
To the light of the sun . . .
To my very own end, of this tragic unmade film.
That I'd shamed the one golden truth that at least . . .
At least . . .
There still may be one more day.
Who's even to say?

May 5th was the second year of the children's art exhibit, just a year since I had received so many phone calls regarding the truck burglary. I was working longer hours and, normally, I would have been at home on that day. I recall that afternoon as I drove home. In the mountains, May is likely to be the first hint of spring. I remember having the car window open and enjoying the fresh warm breeze with a view of the sun setting gloriously over the Wasatch Mountains. It was an orgasmic riot of color, waves of orange rolling across blue. This was Cinco de Mayo, and I had turned down the offer of drinks with friends in a Mexican café. For whatever reason, I just wanted to get home and relax after a busy day. I vividly recall feeling very much at peace that day, driving by green fields and watching the late afternoon glow of receding sunlight. I have never accepted that there wasn't some definite physical sign to me that Brian chose to end his life that day. We were so close emotionally, I cannot understand that I didn't feel something of the pain he was experiencing in making such a difficult decision. I've tried to rationalize that his message lies in the total contentment and beauty of nature I beheld on the day he died.

On Monday, May 10th, the same day the police were trying to locate me, I drove to a small school to display an exhibit of Titanic photos by Adam Jahiel. It was another perfect day that made me feel so happy doing work that I loved. The children were attentive, interested in the photos and asking thoughtful questions. In retrospect, I have felt that Brian's spirit was with me that day, watching over me. It was the last time I will ever feel completely happy and carefree. For several years, it was very difficult for me to be near young children without thinking about Brian or looking for him in each face.

The Austin City police had called Salt Lake City because Brian had a University of Utah identification card. Although he had applied for a Texas driver's license, he had gotten only a temporary card. In their attempts to identify his body, the coroner had removed his fingerprints with no success. The University of Utah gave a reference phone number as Evelyn, the friend who had let Brian live with her while he was finishing his senior year of high school. The police had called Evelyn that Monday and left a message while she was hiking. She returned the call at 4:30 p.m. and gave them my new married name and phone number. The explanation for why they waited until 11 p.m. to call might have been due to an oversight or a shift change. The Park City police chief actually lived on my street. It seems that the local police or the County Sheriff would have been notified first, rather than a random late night call to our home such as we received. I still get anxiety attacks when the phone rings late at night. No matter how long I live, I will never forget the cold, indifferent voice that told me my son was dead.

The greatest irony was that Brian's childhood friend called from Austin the very next morning, looking for him. I'm sure I was very short with him, telling him to call the coroner's office to see Brian. Later, I learned in talking to this friend that he talked to Brian every day, had quit his job in Park City and bought a ticket to go see him two weeks earlier. This fact made me realize how desperate Brian must have been, that he hadn't waited for his best friend's arrival. He was devastated, and we have had several discussions since the incident. He rode back to Park City with one of the others that had lived in the house in Austin. I have never heard from either of the friends Brian had tried to live with in Austin.

STIGMA

had left Brian's care to the people I trusted, his friends, family, even his teachers and counselors as well as many doctors. Because I couldn't cope with his mental illness, I hoped others had either the understanding, patience or knowledge to deal with him better than I did. They didn't. I have said since his death, I wished I had hired a three-hundred-pound man to sit on Brian's chest and force the medicine down his throat. Then again, I do understand and respect that he hated the side effects when he did take the medicine. I am more aware now that it would have rather effectively hindered him sexually, that it would have made him feel nauseous, groggy and lethargic. Even worse, it meant admitting every day that he was mentally ill each time he took that medication. He would have to know that he was different and would never be free of the illness or the medication. He would always feel like a burden to his family and society. Choosing death was his chance for freedom.

Every day I hike along a trail up into the mountains behind our house. It is a path Brian took when he lived with us those few short months. Above the busy freeway intersection and above the houses, there is a beautiful, bird's eye view of the clear river snaking below with its bounty of trout, an attraction to local fly-fishermen and wildlife. An endless range of mountains extends to both the east and the west. The view of the Olympic Winter Park downhill ski jump is a stone's throw, directly to the west. The Olympic jumps will be the focus of world media a half year from now, as I write this.

Once Brian told me he saw a herd of elk grazing over the next hill but was frightened by gunshots around him. I think of that one sentence as summing up his living with one part of his brain in reality and one part in fantasy. Another time I saw him in front of the mirror, making horrible faces. He hated himself and often told me that "people" called him disgusting names. When I asked what people, he looked startled that he had divulged that information and just shrugged, seemingly embarrassed. In his mind, there was an awful world of mean voices that would never be silent. He refused to admit to us that he heard the voices but there were many indications that he suffered their presence. Now I realize how hard he tried to spare us the extent of his illness. In trying to protect us from the truth, he sacrificed himself and his sanity.

I had raised this sensitive, intellectual, poetic, compassionate person who really believed the world hated him. There were times he hated me for bringing him into it. Toward the end of his stay with us, Brian sat beside me on the sofa, put his arm around me with his head on my shoulder and fell into a deep sleep. I sat motionless, enjoying the quiet peacefulness of the moment. Jim walked in and stared at us. When our eyes met, there was some understanding that this time with Brian was so fragile and fleeting. I knew we were losing him.

I have often thought in the past few years, that if Brian had been a football player, his death would never have happened. If he'd been more of a jock and less of a poet, he would have somehow gotten the help he needed. Instead, a sensitive man in our society is looked upon as being weak or lazy. I suspect there were people who thought he was homosexual or simply a drug addict. Besides Sheryl Crow, he loved other women and seemed to fall in love on a regular basis, even romancing the young women at the employment office. He self-medicated with drugs and alcohol which he said made him feel more "normal." But, he also went for months without having any street drugs or prescriptive medicines, leaving him at the mercy of his biologic brain disease.

The stigma I have felt in continuing to live in this small mountain resort town of Park City is overwhelming. People I have known for fifteen years avoid me like the plague. I see them duck down the aisle at the grocery store to avoid me. If I actually talk to them, they hurry to get away. They always say they want to schedule lunch but never do. Although many people attended Brian's funeral, they have since avoided me. And as a result, I avoid them. There isn't much that anyone can do to hurt me any more.

I was very interested to read about Georgia Nucci's loss of her daughter from hepatitis while an exchange student in Ecuador, followed a few months later by her son's death aboard Pan Am Flight 103 over Scotland. As Nucci so eloquently puts it, "When Jennifer died, people were sympathetic. But after Christopher, they started avoiding me. People would turn and walk the other way in the supermarket." She felt some people thought she would bring them bad luck.

My sisters rarely spoke to me for two years following Brian's death, which I assumed was more about them than me. At my father's funeral, my brother only spoke to me in a general way if I happened to be within earshot. He did meet and shake hands with my husband of two years. When my aunt asked about my job in arts and humanities, my brother got up and left the room. She said rather matter-of-factly she was pleased to hear that I'd gotten my life back on track. I wondered if she was referring to my divorce, my bankruptcy, being homeless and moving constantly or my son's suicide. I suspect in her East Texas world she believed that I must have found Jesus and things could be that simple.

I have thought about the stigma issue a great deal. I realize people may intellectually realize mental illness is not contagious, but genetic. With that reasoning, they might still conclude that I might be ill, too. I can tell by a hesitant look in their eyes; they immediately think of their own children and wonder where they are and what they're doing. Seeing me is the reminder of their worst nightmare. It could happen to them, too. Schizophrenia attacks one percent of the entire population of the world, no matter which country or culture. One person in a hundred is ill and affecting the family and friends around them. Yet, we insist on brushing mental illness under the carpet. It reminds me of the saying about the family of an alcoholic not discussing the elephant that is sitting in the middle of the living room. We all just walk around it and pretend it never existed.

As a result, I have become more and more reclusive. I have post-traumatic stress syndrome and find it difficult to work in normal situations. Inevitably, I can't take some situation at work, and then I proceed to blow up or walk out. There is always an underlying anger that my son is dead, and no one understands. I will never receive a gold watch and will always have trouble acquiring insurance benefits. Although I've received some counseling and was offered prescriptions, like Brian, I hate the side effects of anti-depressant medications. The most helpful counseling has been group therapy with others who are suicide survivors or with those who have lost a child. As well-meaning as people may be, they cannot possibly begin to understand how a parent feels in burying their child, out of sync with the timing of nature.

I used to feel sorry for other women distraught over getting divorced – the crying, unhappiness, loss of self-esteem, status and financial support – often over someone they still loved. Until this happened to me, I understood only the tiniest percentage of their grief. The strongest bonds of friendship are now with people who have struggled through a devastating divorce and the loss of a child. I often think it is the culmination of pain that family or employers cannot understand. We aren't just dealing with one isolated loss such as a pet, a job or a hard won anniversary. Surely no one expected that dog to go to law school or bring home grandchildren at Thanksgiving. My new mother-in-law barely missed celebrating her 50th Wedding Anniversary with the death of her husband. That is a huge emotional loss that she earned over a life-time and expected to share with a mate. Although I missed my twenty-fifth anniversary through divorce, I felt robbed of the reward I had earned and fought to preserve. I have learned that grief is different for everyone and there is no official timetable or rational explanation.

As I write this, I am reminded of a story in our local news. A single father had taken his young son, only two years old, on a little road-hunting jaunt. While the boy slept in his car seat, the father apparently got out of the truck and hunted for deer in the nearby area. Certainly not using the wisest judgment, the father didn't realize the boy would awaken, wiggle out of the car seat, unlock the truck door and wander away in search of his dad. Search and rescue parties found the boy after several days, frozen under a light blanket of snow. The judge decided to charge the father with negligence and thirty days in jail. The father eventually returned to the area where his son had died of exposure. On that windy ridge these months later, now July, the father took his own life with the rifle he carried. I don't believe anyone who has not lost a child can understand or should underestimate the tragic grief that burdens a parent. My heart goes out to that Utah family.

The following story is one I wrote after the one-year anniversary of Brian's death. It was published by **Compassionate Friends**, a support group for parents who have lost their children of any age, by any cause. I cannot recommend this group highly enough for their non-judgmental kindness, love and support.

ON THE JOB GRIEVING

This isn't an easy topic several jobs and one year after my son's suicidal death due to the effects of having schizophrenia.

Three years ago I left a telecommuting job with a trade magazine company to accept a position as an exhibition and art education curator. Five months after Brian's death, I walked out of the art center when management problems became overwhelming. It was a job I loved—working with artists, arranging exhibits and scheduling classes. However, I could no longer handle the constant state of depression I felt at the art center. I'd refused anti-depressants, thinking this was some serious hard pain that would soften with time but never disappear. And that is true as I write this.

In my mind's eye, I saw Brian around every corner of the office at the art center where he had visited many times. These were usually his worst moods when he was most demanding of money or hurting from some offhand insult that had upset him on the street. He had raged at me in the office parking lot that the phone number I'd given him for help at the local university was a series of numbers linked to the mafia. The university personnel at the psychiatric hospital had insisted that Brian had to make the appointment himself in order to be helped. He would not make that appointment. Not once do I ever pass that parking lot without seeing the lost, angry confusion in his eyes.

My supervisor, a single woman who was not a parent, was less than sympathetic to my distraction and bouts of emotions and tears. Two days after the funeral in early May, I was asked for the fall schedule of classes. With being hounded over details and funds being cut, I felt I was being forced out the door. On top of all the political power issues going on at work, the building was being remodeled and I developed a constant case of coughing and asthma.

I had read somewhere that it is advisable *not* to quit one's present job during the first year of grieving. Fortunately, at the time I quit, I'd developed two other part time jobs while paying off funeral expenses. I was determined to get the headstone designed and in place by snowfall. This was my last gift to Brian, and it had to be special. By his October birthday, the stone was engraved, placed in the cemetery and finally paid off by Christmas.

One part-time job that summer was editing at a small local newspaper. Unfortunately, the job was hectic—fast paced, highly computerized and stressful so I was relieved to tell the editor I could not stay. Someone at the office said I should get up and jog every morning, that there was no excuse for not jogging. While it didn't make me jog, it still makes me smile. I had also taken on a part-time real estate assistant job that was again too frantic and fractured for my schedule. Trying to keep busy and avoid being alone, I was running my life on a treadmill of jobs. It was so confusing to decide which day it was, what clothing to wear and which office I was going to for the day.

I was numb from the core of my being to the surface of my skin. My muscles turned to jello as my body became less toned and active. On vacation that summer, my husband of a half-year and I drove from St. Louis to East Texas to visit our families. Mine would not mention or acknowledge Brian's death and had not even told any friends, neighbors or relatives. I realize now they were in shock, pain and denial and incapable of reacting in any manner that I needed or wanted for my own comfort. If my own family could not relate to his death, I wondered how co-workers could begin to understand my grief. The young people at the art center had pretended things were normal and had never said a word to me about Brian's death. If I mentioned anything, they quickly became uncomfortable and changed the subject. Fortunately, one person who listened and consoled me was Jim's sister. I poured out my heart and added my considerable amount of tears to her backyard pool.

HOME

Under my doctor's advisement, I got a puppy and decided to stay home for a while to regroup. My mind, body and spirit were exhausted. Sleep evaded me unless I relied on pills. It was all I could do to watch after the twins, a dog, and a cat, plus do anything at all to maintain a household. Some days I could barely force myself to get out of bed and get dressed. It took all my will to get through the day, much less worry about finding another job.

My husband had valiantly taken on a newspaper delivery route to help make ends meet. He continued to do so for over a year, not only for the extra financial boost, but also for the joy of early pristine mornings, glorious mountain sunrises and the chance wildlife sightings of deer, elk, moose and fox. The one thing that would get me out of bed was the guilt mixed with the reward I felt at preparing a hearty breakfast for him.

Incredibly, through a friend, I found another job at a local ski area as fall slipped into winter. I struggled against all odds taking computer classes and handling a highly complex financial program under continual pressure to perform. One day near Christmas, I had to assist on the sales office floor while the sales people were in training. I accidentally tripped on a combination of loose wire, wet tile and a rug. I struck my forehead with considerable force on a low windowsill. Although I felt faint and nauseous, I verbally reported the incident and made it through the rest of the day. There was never any paperwork and the employer could have cared less. The next day, my boss accused me of not being "one of the team" and of not applying myself. I was also told I didn't seem to be "happy" enough. Considering this was my first Christmas without Brian, I had thought I was doing amazingly well keeping my feelings under control. Outside my window at work, the streets were filled with Christmas lights and bustling shoppers. Feeling rejected and emotionally abused, I went home and never went back to that office.

Writing this string of events, I have found the past year to be almost laughable. It has actually been a pretty hysterical six years of being abandoned by my husband of twenty-three years, divorced, alienated from my family, homeless with three children, often unemployed, lacking insurance, declaring bankruptcy, living in low income housing, moving constantly, remarrying and then losing my son to mental illness and suicide.

In almost every employment situation, I felt powerless to control the loss of my job, to gain control of any financial security or insurance benefits, not to mention my self-esteem, to be able to feed my children and not wake up having panic attacks. The boys and I moved nine times in three years before we remarried, and Jim gave us a home alongside a creek where the deer and moose often visited. He promised my twin sons would graduate from high school in this one house, and they have done so with honor and great courage. This summer, they toured Europe and will soon head off to college. I know they are scarred by the loss of their older brother, but they remain strong and focused on the future.

Jim and I worked on making our house into our home this summer. He used a bulldozer to build onto the backyard as I sewed curtains. We found old wrought iron lawn furniture and repainted it. We have painstakingly placed sod on the lawn, planted flowers and trees and just recently created a rock garden. Someday there will be steps down to the creek and a beautiful deck and garden. This kind of work that produces an end result can be so rewarding and helps restore my spirit.

NATURE AND GRIEF

Since January, I have been employed at a park where I coordinate events and act as a fee agent. Under a blanket of snow last winter, I finally found healing in this office and a sense of peace and tranquility that had evaded me the past year. The position is not as challenging or exciting or high-paying as others, but there is a feeling of reward for my accomplishments. My fellow workers are unusually kind, considerate, hardworking and easy to abide. I have not determined whether the changes have been in me or in the situation but they are for the best. I feel Brian's presence in the beauty of nature surrounding me at the park. Although I still grieve for him daily, he remains close to my heart, and I know it is possible to survive his loss.

As I read over this, I note that I left the park for another arts related job. However, the non-profit world is a stressful one in the tough competition for limited funds. Inevitably, I had to leave that job due to recurring anxiety attacks and have returned to writing full time. Optimistically, I don't look at this recent change as another failure. I have moved on to other work that is more rewarding and fulfilling. If I'm not happy with something in my home office, I take the dog for a walk. To be honest, the more I know about the working world, the more I'd rather spend time with my dog. Jim and I will probably move away from Park City soon, away from the hustle and bustle of the Olympics, the increasing traffic congestion and the rising prices. Bear Hollow where Brian once camped and played is now covered with condos. The field where we built our own "field of dreams" and played baseball near the lake where he fished have given way to another housing development. At the cemetery, Brian's grave rests on a hill with a magnificent view of the ski slopes, actually the best real estate deal in Park City. One thing we learn in our grief is that the world carelessly goes on without our loved one. The hopes and expectations of graduations, marriages and new babies continue with each reminder that this could have been a source of joy in our lives, too. But we remain the spectators on the outside, looking in.

During the grieving process, there are many emotions such as a roller coaster ride of denial, anger, hatred, memory loss, lethargy, indifference, impatience and occasional acceptance which are all characteristics of the journey. An obvious reason for the separation from my sisters was the edginess of my temper as we made the funeral arrangements. I recall at the funeral home, one sister was very supportive of the director's idea to dress Brian's body in a jogging outfit. Since I had no doubt he would have to be cremated, I'm sure I looked at them as if they were insane. The director called the Austin coroner and immediately agreed to the better idea of cremation. At the exact time of day Brian's body was cremated, I felt a huge overwhelming sense of grief for the death of the child who had come from my body and that I had nurtured and worried over for twenty-one years.

When Brian's ashes were flown to Salt Lake City, the funeral director initially thought he might be sent by fed-ex, but there was the possibility he would arrive late and miss his own funeral. Instead, we paid for a regular plane ticket so he could attend. When the ashes arrived, there was also a soggy brown paper bag with all of the belongings that had been on his body. It contained his soaking wet watch, his wallet, various business cards, meager identification, pictures of his family and nine cents. I wore Brian's watch to the funeral, then gave it to his father. I've hardly worn a watch since, or cared very much what time it really is. My inner clock is close enough most of the time. The nine cents are framed with his high school track photo and his poem, "A Penny's Worth."

When I saw my sisters pouring over these objects that had been on Brian's body, ones that I had not even seen yet, I became agitated. These were the last items my son had touched. Maybe there was some key, some secret to answer all the questions in my mind. To see them touching his belongings, possibly carelessly destroying those answers, sent me into immediate turmoil. They sheepishly handed me the bag, their feelings hurt. Days later, when Jim had dried out the items, I laid them out on my bed and went over each one, searching to unlock the mystery of Brian's suicide. For many days, I played cd's Brian had given me, *Enya* or *Sarah McLachlan's* songs, as I examined the remnants of his life, looking for clues. Cody finally came to me and insisted there were no answers. I believed him. I put all the pieces away in the closet and rarely examine them.

One issue that came up in the news was the use of a drug called *accutane* which Brian had used to eliminate acne. There is considerable evidence that hundreds of young people possibly suicide after using this drug. It was randomly dispersed to kids with acne and the only warning on the accompanying insert warned against pregnancy at the time of Brian's death. If I had known it was dangerous for someone who was depressed or emotionally unstable, I would never have allowed Brian to use the drug. I assumed the acne was not helping his depression so it made sense to treat it and hopefully improve his self-esteem. He died with clear skin.

The day before the funeral, we drove him home up the mountains for the last time. Brian's ashes were cradled in my arms in a ceramic urn a friend had made at the art center. Brian was now no bigger than when I'd first brought him home from the hospital. I reminisced about the joy I'd felt on a sunny October day in 1977 when we had driven home with him as a baby along back roads shaded by huge oaks overhead in Baton Rouge, Louisiana. His father had been upset by an unexpected detour in the road that day. My parents drove their car practically on our bumper all the way home. My sisters said nothing to this story when I'd finished.

As they got out of the car, I locked the door and sat there holding him and crying uncontrollably. I couldn't stand the thought of having him set in the living room, the object of curiosity as people came and went. Jim placed the urn in our bedroom closet where I could hide the cause of all my loss and grief in private.

When Sam arrived, I forced myself to hug him, despite all the pain he had caused our family. He mumbled something to the effect that at least Brian had brought us back together. I agreed that originally he had. Sam looked ten years older than the last time I'd seen him. That first evening, my sisters disappeared, saying they were going shopping. They had overheard my directions to the condo I'd arranged for Sam and his brother and promptly went over there to comfort them. Hours later I ran into them at the grocery store. I had started my period that day and kept bleeding out of control. Jim had driven me to the store to purchase the necessary feminine articles. When I saw my sisters in the store and realized they had left hours earlier to visit with Sam, I felt once again emotionally abandoned by my family. Some time later, one sister angrily told Cody that I had always tried to control her. She obviously maintained a different perspective on family loyalty and the issue of control under such delicate circumstances.

Some philosophers say we come into this world to fix the one thing our spirit is most lacking and seek out the appropriate parents to fill that void. My issue would certainly have been abandonment. As a child, I continually feared losing my parents. I feared losing teenage relationships and young lovers. As a young bride, I feared the death of my husband. He left anyway. I lost my husband, my child, my father, my home, many jobs and sometimes my health. I would never have thought years ago that I could have survived the loss of any one of these. Each day I am thankful for the blessings I still have, especially for my sons and for Jim. The house and objects mean nothing. It is only the people that are of consequence in the end. When Jim's father or my father died, surrounded by their families, that was all that mattered. The house, the boat, the car, the job – none of it mattered in the least.

Sometimes I think of Brian's philosophies and all he represented and believed in and how he touched so many lives during his short time on earth. He loved his family and home, often entertaining us with his jokes and stories as a young boy. One of his funniest jokes happened on Cody and Dillon's tenth birthday. Their father was insistent on looking at cars for sale before we went to the sports center where their birthday party was to be held and where we would meet the other kids. Brian had gotten a new watch and misplaced it while we were looking at cars. It was raining that day, and we were going back, searching through all the cars that we'd already explored. Finally, we gave up the search to go to the birthday party. Fortunately, the alarm went off, and we found the watch firmly in place on Brian's ankle, rather than his wrist. None of us could stop laughing.

He opened up the world of music, poetry and humanitarian ideas to all of us. Even as a small child, in downtown Salt Lake City, he reached into my purse, grabbed an apple left from lunch and presented it to a homeless man as if it were a gift of gold. Another incident involved a plate of dinner I delivered to him in Salt Lake City. He smiled and handed it to a one-legged, homeless Native American man who was passing by on crutches. I remember that Brian told me that he loved the way I pointed out things like the autumn leaves changing on the mountains. I loved that he exposed the generous humanity he held in his heart. He said·he loved that when I visited our family, he would wake up and hear our voices chattering and laughing in the kitchen. That time has passed.

With such short notice, the funeral plans went well. Many students and teachers turned out in support of my twin sons who were juniors in high school. Their father arrived with his brother from Houston. Long time friends came from California. Although the majority of the time, I felt numb with disbelief, our family greatly appreciated such an outpouring of love and support. It is overwhelming to receive so much affection from so many people in so short a time span. However, after they have left, the silence sets in and you are left alone to cope with your unspeakable grief.

After the funeral, Jim and I went to the hotel where my sisters were staying. I saw them chatting and laughing in a restaurant area with Sam. They had ordered Vietnamese food and suddenly, I was nauseous at the sight of it. My son had died with an empty stomach, and these people were eating and laughing. I turned and ran out the door. They had also brought up the idea that Brian had been murdered for his shoes. As ridiculous as this sounds, I now know people deal with grief differently. Rather than accept the obvious death such as a suicide, they look for someone to blame such as a murderer. The idea that Brian had died from murder only added to my increasing sense of panic.

I personally dread attending funerals and had no idea of the proper format. The things I knew that would be traditionally important to me included the *Twenty-third Psalm*, *The Lord's Prayer* and *Amazing Grace*. The youth minister at the Park City Community Church, also named Brian, sang *The Lord's Prayer* with such incredible emotion that I cried openly, leaning on Jim's shoulder. He sat on my left, Cody, Dillon and their father on my right. I wore a dramatic black netted hat that I thought

Brian would've liked. I pictured Jim and I being married so joyously at the same altar only four months earlier. At each ceremony, the wedding in December and the funeral in May, snowstorms swirled on the mountain landscape outside the tall windows, creating a surreal ambiance. For the wedding, the storm was followed by bright sunlight that shone like diamonds on the freshly fallen snow. For the funeral, it seemed the angels and nature were weeping with us at our loss.

At the altar, a small table held the urn containing my son's ashes. It was decorated with red and white roses, Park City High School's colors. Displayed on the table were Brian's photo when he was running track, his red and white track and cross country letter jacket, a photo album of his childhood and some of his poetry and paintings. It seemed his twenty-one years were represented by this small collection of well-loved phases of his life.

My sister wrote a sweet, touching letter to Brian that was read during the ceremony.

Dear Brian,

My heart is wretched with the sadness of losing you. My pain for our family chokes my thoughts…Today, as we say farewell to our Brian, we should remember the boy who was and the man who would have been; the athlete, the intellectual, and the musician, among so many other gifts.

I clearly remember the very red tiny toes to head baby boy I first met in 1977 in Baton Rouge. Your many photos reinforce the memory of a beautiful child with the sweetest grin and bluest eyes. I remember the August camping trip to Grand Lake when you were about 7; the adult sweatshirts hung long beyond your hands as we lovingly dressed you against the cold morning. I remember the walk we took and the squirrel you found and the Treasure Island we docked the pontoon at so we could play "pirates". Your Mom said you really enjoyed the picture album I sent to you afterwards.

I loved having you visit us; I still have the colored sign that I made for your visits that said, "Brian's Room".

The last time you came to Denver, you surprised me, always so tall and handsome, your blue eyes locking into mine and shying away when I bragged on how handsome you were. I loved you so much. That was the trip when we had birthday cake for all three of you boys, and you all went to the recording studio to make the one of a kind tape, "Live In Denver". You had a song then, unique, just like you.

Brian, if you could see the friends and family here today, remembering you in love, supporting each other in their loss and the many friends from your town and beyond, you would be touched. How did we not reach you with this love you needed? If nothing else, we can vow to ourselves today, in our tribute to you, that from now on, we will recognize the signs of need and never tire to be there for any individual who suffers.

I know you had knowledge of our loving Savior Jesus and those seeds were not planted in your heart in vain. We rest assured that you are in heavenly peace now.

We will never forget you for as long as we live, so no good-byes just, "Eternal peace to you, Brian, sleep well". "Brian's Room" will always hang on my heart.

So much love, Dear Brian,

Aunt Marcia, May 15, 1999

The minister read, "On behalf of Brian's grandfather and Jean's father," a passage from *A River Runs Through It* by Norman McLean.

"Now nearly all those I loved and did not understand in my youth are dead—

but I still reach out to them.

Of course, now I'm too old to be much of a fisherman and now I usually fish the big waters alone although some friends think I shouldn't.

But when I'm alone in the half light of the canyon, all existence seems to fade to a being with my soul and memories—and the sounds of the Big Blackfoot River and a four count rhythm and the hope that a fish will rise—

Eventually, all things merge into one and a river runs through it.

The river was cut by the world's great flood and runs over rocks from the basement of time.

On some of the rocks are timeless raindrops.

Under the rocks are the words and some of the words are theirs.

I am haunted by waters."

Sam's brother read a poem Brian had written a few years earlier.

A Penny's Worth

By Brian Case

One person's life is worth a penny,
And five people, worth five cents.
Some pennies may be dark and rusty,
And some shiny and new.
But when you put all of the pennies in this world together,
Whatever size, color, or age,
You discover that they are all worth the same;
No matter how old or new.
Then put all of the men, women, and children in their world together,
And you discover that life is worth a lot.
Fighting among your enemies, simply because of resources or the color
      of your skin,
Only ends with injured men, and piles of wasted lives.
Always remember, life is too precious to be destroyed.
And if you walk by a rusty penny,
Drowned in a puddle in the middle of the street,
Pick it up and nourish it.
For that child is worth the same as you,
Even if he is poor and homeless,
And needs to steal for a living.
Help the homeless child,
For what goes around comes around,
I have used a penny as an example of life,
One tiny, measly cent-
But in reality
Life is priceless.

The last hymn was one I'd loved for many years. It always reminded me of the spirits of our loved ones soaring up to heaven . . .

"And God will raise you up on eagle's wings, bear you on the breath of dawn, make you to shine like the sun, and hold you in the palm of God's hand."

After the funeral, many people came to our home with plants, flowers and an abundance of food. Our modest home was crowded with friends, relatives and high school kids, including the girls' soccer team still dressed in red and white from their game that Saturday. The students planted a Canadian chokecherry tree in our front lawn. Although nothing grows easily in our rocky soil, that tree has survived and bloomed with flowers each spring and shaded the yard each summer. I often see birds sheltered there. The two anniversaries since Brian's death, a mysterious guest has left roses tied in the tree and containers of flowers around the base of the tree.

Later that afternoon, after the funeral, I went to the garage in search of something meaningful that might be buried along with Brian's ashes. In a box of his baby things, I found a tiny baseball suit he'd worn as an infant. There was a baseball signed by his team and coach when he was about ten years old. I located the running shoes he'd worn not so long ago. I took these items to the cemetery a few hours later. After the minister said a few words, we placed all the items in the container with the urn. I added his favorite poster of Sheryl Crow and a set of cd's by The Doors. He was all set for the next world. As a small group, we stood on that windy hill, snow mixed with early green grass, ready to say our good-byes. His suicide note, which is typical in that it made very little sense as it went on, began with "*Maybe my dying's for the best.*" The word "maybe" has continued to haunt me, that he wasn't really certain this was the answer for him.

At the gravesite, I read a passage I loved from Isak Dinesen's *Out of Africa*. I asked everyone there to substitute deer for lions.

"After I had left Africa, someone wrote to me of a strange thing that had happened by Denys's grave, the like of which I have never heard. "The Masai," he wrote, "have reported to the District Commissioner at Ngong, that many times, at sunrise and sunset, they have seen lions on Finch-Hatton's grave in the Hills. A lion and a lioness have come there, and stood, or lain, on the grave for a long time. Some of the Indians who have passed the place in their lorries on the way to Kajado have also seen them. After you went away, the ground round the grave was leveled out, into a sort of site for the lions, from there they can have a view over the plain, and the cattle and game on it."

I don't remember very much of what happened after that. I tried not to look at the board that covered the freshly dug earth and the hole in the ground, Brian's final resting place. Sam was kneeling on one knee next to the grave. I put my hand on his shoulder and told him that Brian had loved him very much. Everyone was crying. I couldn't stand to watch them put my son into that dark hole. Jim held onto me as we walked to the car. My friend who was driving us asked if we wanted to stay to watch them place Brian in the ground. I began crying hysterically, demanding that we leave. As we drove out the winding road of the cemetery, I looked back and saw people putting pennies in Brian's grave.

A few hours later, we attended a memorial service at the local Catholic Church. I greatly appreciated that they dedicated the mass to Brian as their traditional stance on suicide is not to acknowledge the victim or to allow their burial in a Catholic cemetery. This was a topic that was whispered about when I was young. There was great shame laid on the family and incredible lack of understanding of their grief. Although Brian had served as an altar boy as a child, he had drifted far away from religion. When Cody and Dillon were confirmed at age 16, I remember that it was quite a chore to get the three of them in dress clothes and into church. We took an amusing photo of all our feet toe to toe in dress shoes. Brian stood up for Cody in the ceremony but later told me I should have found someone "better" to represent Cody. I told him no one could be a better choice than a brother.

Brian's poem *A Penney's Worth* is framed and still displayed in a place of honor on a shelf in our living room, along with the nine cents that remained in his pocket when he was found dead. I don't know if pennies were that common before he died, but now I find them in my path everyday. If I am feeling down, then shortly later I will find a penny in the oddest places. It is like a phone call that reminds me Brian is still with us in spirit and lives always in our hearts. It was only when the phone stopped ringing with his calls that I believed he was dead.

TOUCHED

One Sunday last summer, I could not face the pain of sitting in church when inevitably some memory or guilt would set me on the road to endless tears. That day Jim and I decided to build a rock garden from the many rocks around the yard. There is actually an area of unused rock quarry behind the house where the train track ran over a hundred years ago. Robbers camped out in our backyard after they'd looted a train, according to local historians. Occasionally, deer and moose appear out of nowhere on the hillside and come down to drink in the stream.

The reddish rocks are often smooth and weathered by the river, appropriate for surrounding a flowerbed. We patiently collected our favorites and lined the box of the garden area. I noticed a large one that seemed unusual. Jim wrestled it from the earth and found that it was startling in its resemblance to a large fish, even with the markings of eye, fin and tail. We hauled that one to be set near the front door of our house on its own special rock pedestal. Since then, I have placed a terra cotta cherub on its back. Coincidentally, Brian had been especially fond of fishing since he was a toddler. It was a common male bond in our family with his grandfather, uncles, Cody, Dillon and Jim.

As if that wasn't strange enough, finding a fish rock, a huge golden butterfly with a six inch wingspan fluttered down and sat on the rock. Jim and I stared at the butterfly and each other. It stayed quite a while and flew over to some flowers in a pot near the door. I ran to get the camera and actually got a photo of this giant butterfly. I have since learned that some cultures believe they represent spirits of those who have gone before us. After the butterfly left us, I went indoors to return the camera to the shelf. There was music playing that I didn't recognize. I had left the tv playing a rock station on digital cable tv. Now it was on a different channel. As I entered the door, I was greeted by the words, "Hey Jeanie. You are looking for answers in photographs. The answers you're looking for are in nature." I called Jim in to hear this song. Brian often called me "Jeanie" so this really caught my attention. At the time, there were photos strewn around the living room, as I still searched for pieces of the puzzle hidden somewhere in his childhood. He loved to write songs and this sounded like something he'd written especially for me. I realize intellectually this could be a series of coincidences, but somehow, my heart believes otherwise. I know Brian is always with me. I have not been abandoned.

Although there were months that I remained very angry at God for taking my son, I have reached some element of peace with his death. No, I don't believe he had to die. I believe I failed him in many ways due to human error, conflicted emotions and poor judgment on my part. Still, I would not want Brian to continue living in his world of pain and suffering. Reading over his writings reminds me of how hard he struggled to stay with us, how tortuous his life really was. No mother would want her child to continue in such a terrible state of misery. It gives me great comfort to know he sleeps in peace in God's arms.

A wonderful friend and teacher, Mary, explained to her students her thoughts on Brian's suicide. "If a small child was in pain, crying and unhappy, what would you do? You would reach down and pick them up and comfort them. That is exactly what Jesus did. He picked Brian up in his loving arms and took away his pain."

According to the police report, Brian's last words to the clerk at the hostel were,

"Do you believe in forgiveness?"

We forgive you Brian for having to leave us so soon.

We hope and pray you forgive us.

We are so grateful for the time you stayed with us.

In Brian's own words, *Peace out.*

BONANZA YEARBOOK 1996—PARK CITY HIGH SCHOOL

Out of the mouths of babes. I wish I had read these sooner.

Dear Brian,

I will miss you! You've taken one of the few spots left in my heart for very special people. Now I'll want to know how you fare after high school, so you better stay in touch. If I could give you one thing, it would be a look right now through that window into the future where I see you strong, well-loved and happy in your work and relationships. Love, Melissa (high school counselor)

Brian, You are one of the coolest people I know. That letter you sent in to the school newspaper was right on. – Erin

Brian, Try and stay sane. Congratulations on your accomplishments,
– Wyatt.

Brian, It has been extremely fun to have you around. You always make life better. Have a good life, I am sure I will see more of your many movies on national tv – Bryan

Brian, Keep the pony tail, it looks good. I love the videos. Keep on thinking and fighting against walls and enclosures. Stay yourself—you are the greatest. –Alex

Brian, You're a very strange and weird kid, I sort of like that. – Mike

Brian, Thanks for being brave and sharing your oddness with the world. I love encountering it. Also, I like that you are growing and aspiring in your search. Thank you for being profound. Love, Andrea

Brian, It has been really nice figuring out life with you this year. I think you are one of the first real people I've met here, and that is cool. I have really appreciated your friendship. I will miss your awesome writing, your determination to paint and sing, and most of all, to enjoy life. And overall—create your own light, be your own sun. Always, Laura

Brian, I want to thank you first for all your friendship. I always loved talking with you and I'll miss talking with you and I'll miss the hugs. You really are a dreamer, yet so down-to-earth because you know what's really important. Through all that you've endured this year, you are still managing to be a friend to others, to smile when it can be painful. I'll always remember you! May the Lord bless! Always, Jenny

SENIOR QUOTES

Brian Case: "Sometimes I wonder about the creator of the universe."
— Kurt Vonnegut

In the year 2016, I will be . . .

Brian Case: "That's right; I will be, nothing more, nothing less."

BONANZA YEARBOOK 1995

Brian, We always have next year so stop the driving and be safe. Stay the freak and start making movies please. — Brandon

Brian, You are unique. I like that in you. Let your creative tv production carry you far. May the fish be with you. — Kyle

Brian, You are so cool. I wish I had your enthusiasm. Help me get motivated for cross country and track so we can win State.— Chris

Hey Brian, I would say something neat but I just don't have your creativity or your running capability. See ya, Jason

Brian, You're crazy, but I think you're cool! — Alissa

Brian, You're a good guy, Case—You've succeeded in earning my trust, and that is not easily acquired. You have my friendship for as long as I am alive. Much love and trust, John

Brian, Your brilliance blows me away. You're a genius, a saint, a lover. You're too good for this world and all the shit that seems to fall from the skies. Remember, the only way to beat the system is to infiltrate it. You're great. — Taylor

Brian, You're the weirdest person I have ever met. — Jeff

Brian, the fish guy, thank you for the hot sauce and throwing up on the bus 18 times, track is still fun, though. – Alynn

Brian, Who said I can't call you psycho? Befitting—yes; Remembrance— yes; in Admiration, yes; Girl's choice was fun, despite snow and all and I'm glad we went. You make great, entertaining videos and I hope you'll continue. – Jenny

Brian, You're the weirdest guy I know, almost. That's cool. Keep in touch. – Sara

Brian, Truly a weird, weird person. You are really creative. Keep those juices flowing. You are destined for great things. – Rulon

Brian, you are so crazy! Don't let anyone ever tell you that craziness is a negative trait. It is what makes the world go 'round. Stay happy and in your own realm. – Karen

Brian, You are one completely insane guy, but you know what they say. Genius comes with insanity. – Kyle

Case, Sanity is water in your hands. Please drink of it before it slips away because you are one of the few who has direction. Thanks. – Aran

Poem Read at Brian's Funeral -

To An Athlete Dying Young - E. Housman

The time you won your town the race
We chaired you through the market-place;
Man and boy stood cheering by,
And home we brought you shoulder-high.

Today, the road all runners come,
Shoulder high we bring you home,
And set you at your threshold down,
Townsman of a stiller town.

Smart lad, to slip betimes away
From fields where glory does not stay
And early through the laurel grows
It withers quicker than the rose.

Eyes the shady night has shut
Cannot see he record cut,
And silence sounds no worse than cheers
After earth has stopped the ears:

Now you will not swell the rout
Of lads that wore their numbers out,
Runners whom renown outran
And the name died before the man.

So set, before its echoes fade,
The fleet foot on the sill of shade,

And hold to the low lintel up
The still-defended challenge-cup.

And round that early-laurelled head
Will flock to gaze the strengthless dead,
And find unwithered on its curls
The garland briefer than a girl's.

Epilogue

And so our physical lives have gone on without Brian. He continues to live daily in our hearts and souls and spirits. As I write this today, my twin sons have finished their masters degrees, lived, studied and worked all over the world. Despite overwhelming challenges, they have accomplished amazing feats in humanitarian rights and communication through music and language. We are so proud of who they are and the men they have become. The years passed quickly before Jim and I finally left Utah. We spent a year in Northern California, where the ocean and the wine country blend in beauty and bounty. The grassy hills, rocky coastline and blowing sea grasses lent me a year of healing from my pain and guilt. Now we live in the pine forests of East Texas, nearer to our families. Several times, we have visited Austin where Brian lived and died. The lake there remains a peaceful setting that brings a sense of finality and acceptance to my soul. I truly believe God reached down and rescued my son from his tortured existence. I know he is kept safe and sane and someday we will see each other again in a reunion of great joy and many blessings.

Evolving from My Son's Suicide to the Classroom

Within three years after Brian's death, I felt compelled to return to college to earn a masters degree in education. I had watched one of his videos in which he expressed how much his teachers had meant to him. The video touched my soul and reminded me of how rewarding teaching had been in Louisiana when I was young. It had been a dream I'd put on the backburner for many years and relocations. Although I was already teaching during the day in a wilderness school in Utah, I focused on night classes to complete my certification and masters degree. I was fifty-three years old when I graduated.

I've now taught high-risk students in five completely different school settings and find a special symbiotic relationship in guiding troubled students to restore their lives. Although I am certainly no expert, nor do I pretend to be, I do believe I have insight as a parent and teacher into the needs of high-risk and special education students.

The following examples are based on my personal experiences. I specifically do not relate detailed information in order to protect the privacy of those involved.

UTAH WILDERNESS SCHOOL

In the wilderness school environment, I was overwhelmed with finding my way through teaching, counseling, and supporting troubled young adults. I had often worked as a substitute teacher while my sons were in public school. The wilderness school situation was very different and extremely challenging when I was called upon to teach Modern European History, Psychology, Race/Class/Gender, and Shakespeare. My weekends were often busy with school sports and field trips which were especially difficult since I drove to Salt Lake City for classes in the evenings, even through snow storms. However, I loved the school and the students who pushed me to study even harder.

My primary concern was that the administration ruled rather harshly, at least in my opinion. Most of the kids had grown up with everything materialistic but very little attention from parents who were wealthy professionals. The staff consisted of a young, athletic group and the somewhat spoiled, privileged students came from upper class wealthy families. I stood out among the teachers as too mothering and forgiving toward the students' behavior issues. Having recently lost my son, I favored treasuring the moments of their young lives and appreciating the short time they might stay at our school or possibly even stay alive.

I learned a great deal about how therapeutic schools operated and how counseling handled some issues and meds resolved others. Still, there were violent incidences, suicide attempts and extreme behaviors that indicated some of the students were not going to adapt to behavior changes. There were students with obvious mental issues who usually did not remain long in the school and often became runaways. I did not believe the administrators truly understood the difference between premeditated behaviors, acted out behaviors, oppositional defiance and the extreme range of mental illnesses. One routine I abhorred was the teacher lunch time spent bringing forth rebellious students individually onto the red carpet. This humiliation was handled in the teachers' private lunchroom as each teacher in turn stressed the student's faults and mistakes. The process usually ended in students' tears and reminded me of a barbaric stoning that certainly upset the digestive process.

When Jim and I decided to relocate to California, I was relieved to leave the wilderness school and their controlling methods which were in extreme contrast to my own nurturing beliefs. During that time, I thought a great deal about the value of building children's self-esteem rather than annihilating it.

EAST BAY OF CALIFORNIA

Entering a low income California school was an eye-opener for a novice teacher from Utah where we had experienced a ninety-six percent graduation rate. Jim nervously guarded our car at the very rough high school job fair where shabby liquor stores and gun shops resided across the street. This was a shocking reality since we had lived in the pristine land of Zion for a few decades.

I was initially very excited about the challenge of being a certified teacher in one of the worst school areas in California. As initiation, I was handed an "earthquake bag" containing bandages for the entire second floor of the building. That was the extent of my orientation. My class was full of what I would consider extremely emotionally disadvantaged students. When I discussed my concerns with the principal or counselors, I received dismissive eye-rolling that suggested education must have been different in Utah. I was directed to observe a "true" special education class, consisting of a much smaller group of students who were physically impaired and very calm in their classroom environment. By comparison, my students were involved in extreme bloody fights, walkouts, theft, etc. Unfortunately, my students had not been identified as having special needs and were being mainstreamed with no adaptations. More than one of my students would stand and blurt out his restroom needs, then proceed to beat up someone in the hall or restroom. It was nothing short of illegal for the school to treat them with such indifference. They certainly were not receiving the education they needed to progress.

When I was in the school yard, I saw vicious fights where the students crowded around and guards could not physically break through the circle. Students would actually stampede to see blood. I could not believe it when

I saw there were even chain link cages that held desks for the more violent cases. I was nauseated by the conditions and did not remain long in that environment. I felt my hands were tied and that I did not have the power to make any changes. Later, I wrote an article (*San Francisco Chronicle* link below) and appeared on the CBS program *Market Watch* which actually did bring an outpouring of community concern and change.

http://www.sfgate.com/bayarea/article/Why-Johnny-Shakela-and-Jose-can-t-read

HOUSTON, TX

After a disappointing and expensive year in northern California, Jim and I relocated to Houston to be nearer to our families. Our twin sons had finished their studies at the University of Washington in Seattle so there was no need to linger within a day's driving distance. After losing Brian, I had worried even more than normal about Dillon and Cody.

I accepted a job teaching English in Houston at a Juvenile Justice school which housed delinquent teens on their way to jail. There were very few who were finishing their sentences before they could be returned to their home schools. If I'd thought California was a dreadful place for special education, I found that JJ was an even worse placement for high-risk or intellectually disadvantaged students. They were required to walk with their hands behind their backs in single file beneath the lights. Students were thoroughly searched upon each arrival and randomly during the day. Police were always on guard to solve violent outbursts and trained dogs were constantly on campus searching for contraband, especially drugs. I once saw a policeman with a dog take down and handcuff a boy who dropped his napkin at lunch and refused to pick it up immediately. Another incident involved two policeman laughing loudly and labeling two low level learners as "Dumb" and "Dumber" without any concern for being overheard by the students or others.

The worst occurrence was the day I saw a small female teen being dragged downstairs by a policeman. Her face was toward the ceiling with the policeman's arm around her neck. He or she lost the footing on the bottom stair. The back of her head crashed to the floor, splattering blood on my shoes. She was taken to the hospital and remained in a coma for a month. Another incident concerned a boy in my class who had an open wound in his stomach. Blood began pouring through his dirty white shirt onto the floor as he doubled over in pain. When I took him downstairs, the police insisted that I should take him back to class. I refused and said I would take him to the hospital myself. The student was allowed to phone his grandmother who told him she was too drunk to drive. Finally, the administrators determined they would return him to the prison hospital so his wound could be addressed.

I was particularly sorry for the situation of the students who were simply being warehoused until prison became their full-time home. Many had never been required to attend classes as their education was apparently optional. Most of these students read at a first grade level or not at all. Either due to their many emotional and traumatic life experiences or undiagnosed disabilities, or their lack of a nurturing, healthy environment, the chances they could overcome their disadvantages were bleak. Unbelievably, I've also taught bright teens to read who were required to stay home through their childhood to care for a grandparent or other relative. These deprived children had never attended school through no fault of their own. Their education had illegally been withheld from them.

Teen pregnancy was another major problem, often complicated by being the result of rape or incest. I overheard one pregnant girl who planned to have her baby being confronted by an extremely angry female student. The situation was escalating and they were ready to ball up their fists when the pregnant girl took control. She patiently explained that at sixteen, she'd already had three abortions. Her doctor had told her she might not ever have a live baby if she had any more abortions. I was relieved to see the two girls resolve their issues and listen to what each other had to say.

With cutbacks, there were fewer police the next year along with an increased student population. Students' rage erupted daily in more and more extremely violent acts and attacks. Anything could be a weapon— a stapler, scissors, a computer, a pencil, a desk. Eventually, portable buildings were added to accommodate the growing population. Then students began to climb in and out of windows and have sex in any empty classroom.

My walkie-talkie disappeared and had been hidden in the ceiling tiles of the restroom. Fortunately, it was still on the next morning and spoke to me from above the toilet. I felt better when I learned that the new policeman's car keys were stolen and sealed behind a loose brick on the outer wall of the building. Despite their disabilities, the students had quick hands to steal, pass drugs or lock a teacher out of the room. Teachers had to be on survival mode at all times. The stress level was extremely demanding.

Once the principal, who was very strict and generally disliked by both students and staff, decided to verbally discipline all of the students at lunch. She made the mistake of angrily asking, "Do you think that's funny?" All it took was for one student to respond, "Hell yeah!" Others joined in a chorus and the room became pure chaos as one large girl hooked her arm around the principal's neck. She dragged the smaller principal with her high heels making odd little bouncing movements as the student made her way across the gym to a corner. I noticed many of the staff had to stifle their smirks to keep straight faces. I made a mental note to never ask an open-ended ridiculous question to a mass of kids in a volatile situation such as the one I had witnessed.

The Juvenile Justice environment taught me many things: that there was little justice where students were concerned, that the system primarily warehoused mentally ill youth until they somehow ended up in the prison system, that they are often deprived of an education through no fault of their own, and that their family system has disintegrated to the point that even the state could not ensure a decent education and their future survival.

I remember a female teen who continually slept in class. Finally, after much encouragement, she admitted that her uncle forced her to work at a strip club most of the night which resulted in lack of sleep. She added that he also kept most of the money she earned. These teens acted the way they had been taught or treated others the way they had been treated whether it was through molestation, fighting, verbal abuse or any number of ways that have been used to hurt humans and exploit children. There are so many stories that I still carry in my heart and pray for those young people who by now are trying to find their way in the world.

I've experienced teaching special education in two other Houston schools. One was in a regular educational school which was low income, overcrowded and mismanaged by a continual turnover of administration. Although there were many loving, involved, hard-working parents, teachers and staff, there were administrators that would have preferred to simply sweep the special education department not only under the carpet but out the door. The main reasons for their disdain of special ed were the time-consuming paperwork and the annoying problem of special students failing standardized testing. When special ed scores were included with regular students, the overall results were usually lower, thus influencing the data that is the foundation of all that is wonderful in the regular ed world. Data driven evidence means everything to school districts. Basically, the bottom line is money along with school recognition labels such as "Blue Ribbon" or "Excellence" rather than standard labels.

Many administrators have little to no compassion or understanding of what life is like for the parents who struggle to get their children to school or afford medicine and equipment. Even if the parents can understand the laws and language as well as fill out required, complicated paperwork for the lunch program or other assistance, there are often glitches with social workers and standards that prevent poor people from qualifying for the help they need. Sometimes undocumented immigrant parents fear deportation and will not reveal financial information. I learned that the need for equipment such as a child's wheelchair may be ignored because a parent is not a U.S. citizen and fears deportation. In one situation, the old chair was worn out and too small for the growing child. As a result, the unfortunate child was forced to suffer without the dignity of having proper equipment.

In my experience with the regular ed schools, there are often difficulties for parents who are incapable of advocating or finding support in the fight for the rights of their special needs child. Some parents in our state and others, lack not only the language, but the speaking skills or ability to express their concerns even through an interpreter. We have a continual influx of immigrant children who may have a speech, hearing or visual impediment and also be struggling with their native language. The fact that the students have additional special needs such as bipolar disorder may be overlooked completely due to the more obvious communication problems. A student may go for months or even years before they are correctly diagnosed if they are shuffled into crowded classrooms with overwhelmed and frustrated teachers.

Any parent, who is aware of discrimination against their child due to a public school not meeting their student's needs, has every right to seek legal assistance and advocacy. Often, schools are reluctant to deal with law suits and will settle fairly with parents who hire an advocate or attorney to represent the child. Of course, most interventions would require payment by the parents which is another reason lower income families are often not able to hire a consultant. Immigrant parents often work several jobs at the cost of family time. Besides the obvious financial stress, parents face problems getting time off work to visit the schools for conferences.

Sadly, I have encountered suicidal parents as well as students who were no longer able to cope with their extreme conditions. Incredibly, I was once reprimanded for counseling a suicidal student at the request of the parent. Instead, I was told to attend a meeting regarding events that would not occur until several months later. School counselors may be so overburdened with paperwork and standardized testing results, there is little time spent actually counseling. Clearly, there is considerable room for improvement in the system when children are put on a backburner, silently waiting for help.

Although I could relate endless incidents of injustice toward special needs children by the legal, educational or medical systems, I simply want to bring attention to the desperate need for compassion and advocacy. If readers possibly have gained enlightenment or understanding of the discrimination people with mental illness and their families experience, then I believe my purpose in writing this book has been achieved. Even more so, if readers will take that information, research further, and apply the findings in their own lives, they will be able to synthesize what they've learned. This last step will prove more valuable and productive for incorporating the special needs population into our society.

PREVENTION AND NURTURING

1. Educating teens and adults before pregnancy

Although it may be obvious to some readers, there are so many females who do not realize that during their reproductive years, the damage caused by drugs, alcohol or toxic chemicals–smoking, lead paint, cat litter, and dangerous fumes can cause insurmountable problems for their offspring later in life. Teens and adults need to be made aware that a high risk lifestyle can be directly related to causing birth defects. Follow up child care training and education after the birth are essential, too. For example, so many tragedies could be avoided by warnings not to leave a baby in the care of a jealous boyfriend or unreliable babysitter, friend or relative. I've witnessed the tragic results in traumatic brain injuries (TBI) that can destroy a child's ability to learn and process thoughts. Another step in avoiding disaster is as simple as reminders to check the interior of a vehicle to avoid leaving a child abandoned and alone. A reminder can be to leave a purse or phone near the child rather than have the child die of extreme weather or suffocation. Just as they need to be watched in the proximity of pools or receive immunizations, our children need to be protected from an over-stimulated society that actually leaves babies in cars. Please advise any relative, friend or acquaintance of the numerous dangers causing physical and mental disabilities or even death that are completely avoidable through education! Do not overlook your responsibility to report suspected harm or irresponsible treatment to any child through Child Protection Services (CPS). Yes, you can report anonymously.

2. Health Checks

Unfortunately, all students do not get the help they need regarding physical matters, even those as simple as sight and hearing checks. I've experienced how difficult it is for students to learn without being able to see or hear, especially when they have not been identified as needing modifications. A pair of glasses can go a long way in assisting a struggling reader. Additionally, pre-natal care is a huge benefit to the unborn baby who may be suffering from lack of nutrition or exposure to harmful substances. It would seem obvious to anyone reading this book that pregnancy is a huge responsibility in bringing a human life into this world. Again, if you know of anyone who needs help with finding resources for prenatal care, please follow through in helping them find assistance. Not every pregnant teen knows who to turn to or who to trust. Be that dependable person to give guidance and help to the young mother or father. You can contact a variety of social services through your educational, medical, legal or religious community.

3. Intervene

Be available for those who cannot help themselves. If someone you care about, love or know is on a road to self-destruction, and possibly the destruction of the health of their baby, try to re-route them to get rehabilitation or whatever help they may need. There are many online or phone resources in most communities. Assistance may be reached through churches, clergy, hotlines, medical sources and many educational and governmental resources. If you don't know where to access help, visit your local librarian. In my opinion, "tough love" is a theory that rarely accomplishes anything except the return of an angrier, more confused and distressed young adult who holds less trust and hope for the future.

4. Fight Bullying with education

Another way everyone of us can intervene is to stop any form of bullying that we may hear about or witness. My students have suffered terribly in regular ed schools while being held in contempt for *involuntary tics*, such as eye movements, *flat affect* or lack of facial response, and *stemming* which is continually focusing on the movement of one object such as a pen or paper. Even teachers who are unaware have asked to have students removed from class for the former, not realizing these are physical aspects of mental illness or side effects of medications and beyond the student's control. We all need to fight the stigma of mental illness through education and awareness. Most importantly, all of us should remember to teach each other tolerance of all who are different and actually celebrate the uniqueness of individuals for whatever reason.

5. Observe

Observation cannot be emphasized enough. Parents, relatives, teachers, and other professionals are all called upon to participate in raising healthy children. Be aware of changes in personality, school and home behaviors, poor treatment of smaller children or animals, sexual acting out, poor hygiene, drug use or other addictions, writings or any other indicators that tell your subconscious to take note. It is often so easy in our busy world to overlook the obvious. If the neighbor's children are ragtag and hungry, along with running the streets at all hours, the family obviously needs help. If a person talks about suicide, listen closely. Even if there is no intention, there is some unmet need for attention that the person is trying to express. Does the person have a thought out plan? Ironically, I overlooked Brian's obvious pleas for help in his writing out of respect for his privacy. Today, I give each of my students a journal as a barometer of their mental health. The topics they choose to write or draw upon are an indicator of their many issues.

6. Support the rights of the mentally ill - Advocate

Whether the mentally ill person is a member of your family, a student, neighbor or friend, educate yourself on the rights of the mentally challenged. Perhaps you can initiate a way to fight stigma in your community through the schools, medicine or law. Advocate for those who cannot speak for themselves. Support the **National Alliance for the Mentally Ill (NAMI)**. Walk through assisted living for the elderly and see if there isn't something you can do to fight *Alzheimer's* disease and bring mental disease out of the darkness. Notice the A.D.A. ramps available in every public building and think of ways to build that ramp for the intellectually disadvantaged.

7. Volunteer or mentor

Whatever free time you might have at some point in your life, there is always a need to fill for community volunteers. Teaching a young child to read is much easier than teaching a sixteen-year-old who reads on a first grade level. You could change a young person's life by donating or volunteering through community organizations, schools, recreational environments, park services, religious settings and many others. Again, your local library may be a resource for finding the volunteering position that meets your skills. There is nothing like serving in a soup line or assisting Habitat for Humanity to help you appreciate your own life circumstances and realize how fortunate you are. Certainly, offering helpful advice for those in need, if you are qualified, would be an excellent use of one's counseling, medical or legal expertise.

Finally

On behalf of Brian and the many intellectually disadvantaged children in our schools, homeless people in the streets, mentally ill prisoners and all who suffer with brain disease, I ask that you stop and ask "what if" that person could possibly be your own child or spouse or parent. Would we all be so annoyed with stepping over the homeless if that person were one of our family or friends? Would we be so determined to inflate standardized test scores to represent the gifted but ashamed to account for the lowest achievers? Would we accept imprisoning and purposely punishing people who are mentally ill? Or would we all be so oblivious to voting for reliable politicians who would sincerely work to resolve some of these issues?

I know that it isn't a perfect world or Brian would be here with me right now, editing my mistakes and laughing at my somber thoughts. His doctors said he "fell through the cracks" in the system. Let us all work together to fill in the cracks, improve the system, break it down and rebuild the system, or whatever it takes so that other families will never get that phone call in the dead of night.

about the author

Jean Baker is a Special Education English and Reading teacher who continues to advocate for children with special needs. Her twin sons, Brian's younger brothers, have lived and studied in England, Ghana, Tunisia, Sudan (Darfur and Yambio), France, Canada, Kosovo and Kyrgyzstan. She loves to travel to visit them as well as expand her writing horizons. She lives with her husband Jim and two dogs in Houston, Texas. She also cares for her elderly mother with Alzheimer's disease, but that is another story.

16598885R00231

Made in the USA
Charleston, SC
30 December 2012